Nic

God bless you.

PUT SOME GRATITUDE IN YOUR ATTITUDE!®

It was great
meeting you! Keep
Hope Alive!

Your Friend,

Roy Johnson

5/29/08

PUT SOME GRATITUDE IN YOUR ATTITUDE!®

Roy Johnson

PUBLISHED BY:
BRENTWOOD CHRISTIAN PRESS
4000 BEALLWOOD AVENUE
COLUMBUS, GEORGIA 31904

TABLE OF CONTENTS

DEDICATION

This book is dedicated to the wonderful memory of all of my deceased family members and friends who helped to inspire and to motivate me in some way during the course of their lives. Some of them are: my father Elder William Johnson, my son Ray Johnson, my sisters, Brenda Louise Johnson and Edna Clayborn, my brothers, DeArthur Johnson and Theoplis Johnson, my nephew, Samuel Jordan and my uncle and aunt, Elder and Mrs. C.L. Benton who helped to raise me. This book is also dedicated to the memory of my mother-in-law, Mrs. Lillie Pearl Page and her sister, aunt Bessie Blake, my brother-in-law, Wilmer Page, Jr. and to my good friend and physician Dr. Raymond P. Miller, Sr. Dr. Miller helped to care for me during my illness. He passed away in 2005. It is also dedicated to the memory of Deacon Davis Young, Mother Lee Ollie Savage and Mother Erma Withers. I also dedicate this book to the memory of Judy Chappell, a good friend and former co-worker who inspired me by introducing me to the phrase, "TODAY IS THE TOMORROW THAT WOR-RIED YOU YESTERDAY AND ALL IS WELL"! I adopted the "ALL IS WELL" and this is what God used to help me through the major illness that I experienced in 1994 and 1995. Each one of you will forever hold a special place in my heart, and I will never ever forget you!

ACKNOWLEDGEMENTS

I first give praise and honor to God, His Son Jesus Christ and the Holy Ghost or the Holy Spirit for inspiring me to write this book. I also thank God for allowing me to experience one of the greatest opportunities that I have ever had in my life. The opportunity of knowing what it is like to be counted out and then to see God step in and turn things around for you. Dermatomyositis, the rare disease of the muscles and skin that attacked my body in 1994 and 1995, was a blessing in disguise.

I would like to give special, special thanks to Marie, my wonderful and beautiful wife of 32 years, for her love, her patience and for the wonderful care that she gave me throughout my illness and for her patience and the encouragement that she has given me over the years as I have worked on this book.

I would also like to thank my son Eric Johnson, who is now 28 years old, and my daughter Eboni Johnson, who is 24, for the wonderful care that they gave me during my illness.

Special thanks to my brother Charles Johnson and his wife Diane of Detroit, MI for all of their encouragement and the hard work that they put into the development of this book. Special thanks also go to all of my other family members who helped to encourage and to inspire me during my illness. Their names are mentioned throughout the book. They are: my father Elder William Johnson, who passed away in December 1998, and my wonderful mother, Mrs. Laura Johnson, who is 92 years old. Also James and Ozetta Johnson, Clint and Sharon Johnson, William and Peggy Johnson, Queen Esther Ganaway, LaTrese Johnson Martindale and her daughter Brooklyn Johnson, Samuel and Nell Johnson, the late Edna Clayborn, Preston and Margaret Johnson, Freddie Ray and Johnnie Johnson and Oliver, Laverne and Oliver Haney III.

Special thanks also go to my wonderful and beautiful granddaughter Keyona "KiKi" Johnson, who is three old. Although she was not around during my illness, the joy that she brings has been a great source of encouragement to me in the completion of this book.

I would like to thank the entire staff of St. Vincent Infirmary Medical Center in Little Rock for the great care that they gave me during my illness. Special thanks to all of my doctors who were there for me. They were: the late Dr. Raymond P. Miller Sr., Internal Medicine. Dr. Miller was my family doctor, and he was there for me all the way. It was Dr. Miller who first suspected that I had a muscle disease. I was referred to Rheumatologist, Dr. Christopher Adams for treatment of the disease. Dr. Adams did a wonderful job of caring for me during my hospital stay and after-wards for annual checkups. He has since moved out of state. Many thanks go to my other wonderful doctors who were very instru-mental in my care. They were: Dr. David Rozas, Ophthalmologist; Dr. Coburn Howell, Neurologist; Dr. Gordon Gibson, Neurologist; Dr. Robert Abraham, Neurosurgeon; Dr. Joe Pevahouse, Kidney Specialist and Dr. Joe Hargrove, Cardiologist.

Special thanks to Ms. Margaret Washington. She was the nurse that was assigned to care for me my first night in the hos-pital. She was there for me when many thought that I wouldn't live through the night. Many thanks to all of the other nurses and staff who did a wonderful job of caring for me while I was hos-pitalized. Many thanks also go to my nieces and nephews Earl and Diane Jordan, Calvin and Debra Johnson, William and Brenda Johnson, Brenda Meade McIntyre and Dr. Yolaundra Yvonne Meade-Williams.

I would also like to give special thanks to my pastor, Elder Jewel Withers Jr. and his wife Joyce and the entire Williams Temple Church of God In Christ family. They were absolutely wonderful in caring for me and my family during my illness.

Special thanks go out to former Superintendent of the Conway Human Development Center where I work, Mr. Bob Clark and for-mer Assistant Superintendent Mrs. Carol Shockley, Mrs. Carolyn Coney, former personnel director, and to all of the employees of the Conway Human Development Center past and present. Everyone was so supportive of me during my illness and afterwards. Mr. Clark and Mrs. Shockley gave me my first opportunity to speak at a major regional training conference sponsored by CHDC. The name of this conference is "Beyond The Borders". They also gave me opportunities to speak at other training conferences that really helped to launch my speaking career.

Special thanks also go to present CHDC Superintendent Mr. Calvin Price and Assistant Superintendent Ms. Marilyn Junyor along with Ms. Gail Miller, Mr. John Duffie, and Ms. Kathy Guffey. They have continued to ask me to speak at "Beyond The Borders," which has given me a lot of confidence when I speak at other conferences around the country. Mr. Price also has been very supportive of my speaking career by approving many requests from persons who ask me to speak to their groups. Special thanks to CHDC Chaplain George Andrews, who visited me on a regular basis, and gave me a lot of encouragement.

I would like to thank Arkansas Department of Health and Human Services director Mr. John Selig and former DHHS director Mr. Kirk Knickrehm and Ms. Julie Munsell for allowing me to travel around the state with them to promote the services offered through DHHS. Thanks also to Developmental Disabilities Services director Dr. Charlie Green and former DDS director Mr. Mike McCreight for their support and encouragement over the years. Special thanks also go to Mr. Forrest Steele, Superintendent of the Jonesboro Human Development Center and Ms. Cheryl Willie, who always encourage me by asking me to do motivational sessions for their employees.

My former supervisors in staff development Mr. Ed Jennings and Mrs. Mary Jane Russell also were very supportive of me, during my illness and afterwards. My current supervisor Mr. Stuart Douglas is also very supportive of me and he encourages me to use the talents that God has given me.

Special thanks go to my friends Supt. David Withers and his wife Cora, Lisa Gamble, Kaye Malcom, Jo Battle, Jo Nalley, Ron Barnett, Stella Morris, Tony Mock, Loisetta French, LaShana Shelton, Virginia Brigance, Joyce Credit, Teresa Shaw, Ella Marks, Joe and Rosemary Winford and to my many other friends who have been a great source of encouragement to me concerning my motivational career and the worldwide tour.

I would like to thank all of my co-workers in staff development and dietetics past and present who have encouraged me so much over the years. The ones that I have the pleasure of working with now are: Stuart Douglas, Kellie Wilson, Lisa Koch, Jill Blankenship, Jana Lockhart, Alesia Holbrook, Melinda Ross, Kevin Bowman, Jennifer Evans, Marsha Brown and all of the employees of the Conway Human Development Center.

Special thanks go to my adopted sister, Dee Swift who now lives in New Jersey. Dee was very helpful to me during my illness and made several calls to check on me when she lived in Dallas, TX. Dee also introduced me to the internet and to e-mail. She developed my first internet website and also developed my e-mail address, which is Roystest@aol.com. Roystest stands for Roy's testimony. Before I was blessed with a computer, Dee would receive my e-mail on her computer and mail it to me. I was discussing this process of how I got my e-mail with a great friend and co-worker Dwight Sowell and he chuckled for a moment and then he told me that she could e-mail it to his computer and he would print it off for me and I could get same day service! Praise the Lord! Now since I have a computer I have the capacity to receive and send e-mail from my own home!

Liz Massey and her cameraman John Dodd of KTHV-11 television station in Little Rock deserve special recognition for an interview that they did on me and showed it on "Everyone Has A Story". It talked about the worldwide tour and how God miraculously healed me of the muscle disease. After it aired I began to get calls from people from around the state of Arkansas and also from Oklahoma.

Liz and John did a great job! Special thanks also to Anne Jansen of KTHV, who made sure that my mother got a copy of the interview.

Special thanks go to Corey Oliver for his review of the manuscript and also special thanks to my good friend Kellie Wilson for her typing and review of it.

Thanks so much to Bishop Cornelious T. Fountain of Jersey City, NJ for encouraging me to complete the book and to continue my travels on the worldwide tour. I would also like to thank Mr. Larry Mitchell from San Antonio, TX for his encouragement and support. We met about two years ago at Dallas Love Field Airport. I walked up to him, introduced myself and shared my testimony with him and gave him a brochure on PUT SOME GRATITUDE IN YOUR ATTITUDE!® My good friends Rev. O.D. Phillips and his wife Carolyn and Rev. David Gober and his wife Dorothy deserve special thanks for always encouraging my ministry.

Thanks also to Roy Kindle, Mary Cross, Julie Goodnight, Regina Price, Mary Short, Ralph Nelson, Dawn Martin, Tina Brown, Betty Young, Ne'Nita Clayborn, Carolyn Wade, Mary Jones, Alberta Blakely, Doyle Parker, Jo Ann Jones, Kim Fountain Tidwell, Sarah Hunt, Jackie Brigance, Doris Rigsby and to Barbara Grant of Detroit, MI for always being there to encourage me.

My father-in-law Mr. Wilmer Page Sr. also deserves a special thanks for always being there to encourage my ministry and the worldwide tour. The entire Page family is to be highly commended for the care and encouragement that they gave me during my illness.

Many thanks to Bishop L.T. Walker, Jo Ann Matthews, Clara Shoemaker, Brother Loyd White, Larry and Donna Terry, Lawson Pilgrim, Kenny and Loyce Griffin, Becky Jorgensen, Floyd Morrow, Cynthia Thompson, George McCray, Mark Hill, Bruce Allen and Sister Dorothy Barnes for their encouragement and special thanks to Gina Lowe for referring me to my publisher.

Thank so much to all of you that I was not able to mention by name but who have always been there for me. May God continue to bless each one of you!

Roy Johnson
Little Rock, Arkansas

INTRODUCTION

PUT SOME GRATITUDE IN YOUR ATTITUDE!® is a true story about the trials and triumphs that I experienced in 1994 and 1995 with "dermatomyositis". This is a rare disease of the muscles and it also affects the skin. This book tells of how God miraculously healed me of this disease. No traces of it have been found since. PUT SOME GRATITUDE IN YOUR ATTITUDE!® illustrates how God gave me the strength in the midst of the storm to "PUT SOME GRATITUDE IN MY ATTITUDE"!

Are you grateful, thankful, and appreciative to God for what you have and for things being as well as they are for you or do you constantly complain about what you don't have rather than being grateful for what you have? If you are not as grateful as you ought to be you need to PUT SOME GRATITUDE IN YOUR ATTITUDE!®

Anything can happen to any of us at anytime, suddenly and without warning. It doesn't matter who we are or what we have. How will you handle it if something does happen to you or someone that you love? Will you give up and throw in the towel? Will you lose faith in God? Will you stop serving him? Well, you don't have to but you can PUT SOME GRATITUDE IN YOUR ATTITUDE!® The rare disease of the muscles and skin attacked me suddenly and without warning in 1994 but God gave me the faith, strength, and courage to "count it all joy." James chapter 1 verses 2-3 says:

(2) My brethren, count it all joy when we fall into divers temptations;

(3) Knowing this, that the trying of your faith worketh patience.

Many of us are not very grateful, thankful and appreciative for what we have until we lose it. It seems as though it takes losing something that is of value and something that is dear to us in order for us to appreciate it. I would like to encourage you to value and appreciate what you have now because the next second it could be taken away from you. In times of difficulty and adversity rather than running from the answer we need to run to the answer! I knew that the answer to the very rare and debilitating muscle disease that I experienced was in the power of God. So, therefore, I was grateful, thankful and appreciative to God for things being as well as they were for me because I knew that God didn't allow it to happen to me to make me bitter but to make me better!

I was persuaded that God was able to deliver me from the muscle disease, but if He chose not to, my heart was fixed and my mind was made up to continue to serve Him anyway, NO MATTER WHAT! I was convinced as Shadrach, Meshach, and Abednego were of what they told king Nebuchadnezzar after he had made threats to throw them into the burning fiery furnace for not serving his gods and for not bowing down to worship the golden image that he had set up.

They responded to the king in Daniel chapter 3 verses 17-18:

(17) If it be so, our God whom we serve is able to deliver us from the burning fiery furnace, and he will deliver us out of thine hand, O king.

(18) But if not, be it known unto thee, O king, that we will not serve thy gods, nor worship the golden image which thou hast set up.

They were thrown into the burning fiery furnace for disobeying the king's orders, but God delivered them even in the midst of the fire.

A good friend of mine, the late Deacon Davis Young would always say, "from the time you are born to the time you ride in a hearse things are never so bad that they couldn't be worse"! This helped me to PUT SOME GRATITUDE IN MY ATTITUDE!

God has allowed great causes and great movements to be born through people who have experienced tragedy and adversity in their lives. You don't have to give up when things happen to you but you can put it all in the hands of God and in due time He will bring you through. You have to keep the faith and be strong and of good courage. I was an eyewitness to the events that you will read about in this book, and I recorded them as I was inspired to do so by the Holy Spirit.

The purpose of this book is to encourage you to always try to find something to be thankful and grateful for even in the midst of your trials and even in the midst of life's most difficult situations. I have personally discovered that it is the difficult times that we face in life that offers us the greatest opportunities to grow and to become all that God wants us to be. He knows what is best for us and He knows what we will have to face up the road before we get there. He will prepare us for those things if we will allow Him to. I have a quote on my office walls that says, "I would rather walk in the dark with God than to go alone by sight". Another one says, "The man who walks with God will always get to his destination".

The majority of this book was written from my hospital bed, room 2344, St. Vincent Infirmary Medical Center in Little Rock, Arkansas. I was there from December 30, 1994 until February 2, 1995. I started writing this book immediately after being admitted to the hospital. It has taken eleven years for it to fully develop, but I am convinced that God is never late but He is always on time!

I was diagnosed on December 30, 1994 with dermatomyositis. I was 44 years old. I also developed a condition called Rhabdomyolsis, which basically means a melting away or a disintegration of the muscles. My CPK, or muscle enzyme level, was over 30,000 points. The normal range is around 250 points or below. I am now 55 years old with no signs that I have ever had the disease, and I am not on any medication for it. I was admitted to the hospital the same day that I was diagnosed with the disease. I had gone to several doctors for six months prior to this time. By this time I was almost dead and had become physically disabled. This book was written in the midst of the most ferocious storm that I had ever experienced. I had never been so ill in my life. In spite of it all, God had prepared me for this illness. Twenty years before I was diagnosed with this illness, I had given my life to Jesus Christ on September 1, 1974, and had accepted the call to preach the gospel on December 29, 1974. This foundation that God had given me is what I depended on to get me through the illness. My condition deteriorated on a daily basis during the month of December 1994. Just getting out of bed became a very difficult task. By this time my legs, hands, and feet were severely swollen. I could barely dress myself. My wife had to give me a great deal of help. I could barely raise my leg from the floor, and I could no longer button my shirt up without assistance. It would take me over two hours to get cleaned up and to get dressed to go to work. Believe it or not I worked up until December 22, 1994, eight days before I was admitted to the hospital. It was only by the grace of God that I was able to do this. One morning while taking a bath, I suddenly realized that I did not have the same strength that I had the day before. After I had made a valiant attempt to get out of the bathtub, I suddenly realized that I couldn't do it. In an effort not to let my wife and children know how weak and feeble that I had gotten, I struggled for about thirty minutes trying to get out of the tub. Each time I thought I was almost out, I would slip back down in it. Finally, as I struggled and struggled, God gave me the strength to get out. Praise God! Needless to say, it was a long, long time before I tried getting in the tub again. I then went to taking showers until I had gotten too weak to do that, but "ALL IS WELL"! During this time the doctors were still running tests to determine what was wrong with me. They were running the same test that they would have run if I had been in the hospital. By the time that I entered the hospital, I had gotten to where I could no longer walk, comb my hair, raise my hands up past my shoulders or hold my head up. Overall I was in a very weakened and deteriorated condition, but thanks be to God, I still had breath in my body! Psalms 150:6 says: "Let everything that hath breath, praise the Lord. Praise ye the Lord."

Praising the Lord is what I began to do. Not asking him "Why me?" But rather," Why not me?" I started answering the telephone in the hospital by saying, "Praise the Lord!"

As I entered the hospital I asked God to show me what I could do for Him as I lay at death's door. I knew that there was a purpose for me being in the condition that I was in. I also knew that God didn't allow it to happen to me to make me bitter, but to make me better! My first night in the hospital God spoke to me and told me to start a midnight revival service from my hospital bed and I did! I turned my hospital telephone into a prayer line. The prayer line was open from 6:00 A.M. until 9:30 P.M. I also started a radio ministry from my death bed by way of Elder Paul Robinson and Elder Jerry Bradden, who have radio broadcasts. God miraculously healed me of that disease and then he told me to start a worldwide tour and share my testimony with others. In January 1996, I started the worldwide tour by going two blocks from home. I then went about five miles from home and then about 20 miles from home. I also took the worldwide tour to a place in Arkansas where the population is about nine people. Everywhere I went I was proclaiming that I was on a worldwide tour, telling others about the miracle that God had given me. By this time my critics had observed that the worldwide tour had only taken me to a few places here in Arkansas. They begin to question the validity of the worldwide tour since I had only been just a few miles from home. I expressed to them that God didn't tell me to finish it at this time, but He told me to start it and I started it! I also expressed to them that "a journey of ten thousand miles must first begin with one step"! I made that one step of faith and now it is January 2006, and God has blessed me to travel to almost all of the fifty states, to over 200 cities, and I have traveled to other countries. Praise God!!

During the time of my illness I always used the phrase "ALL IS WELL"! You will see "ALL IS WELL" as the recurring theme throughout this book. This was a great consolation to me during my illness, and it helped me to maintain my faith in God even in the midst of the storm! It helped me to be content, grateful, and thankful in my heart and spirit that God allowed me to have this great opportunity to be used by Him. To God be the glory! Whenever someone would ask me how I was doing, my response would be an emphatic "ALL IS WELL"! I responded this way regardless of how I felt or looked or of the bad news that I was receiving from the doctors or the discouragement that I was receiving from those who really didn't understand the power of God. After I witnessed God's awesome power over the muscle disease "ALL IS WELL" was transformed into "ALL IS WELL AND THEN SOME". This became my new slogan until God transformed it into ALL IS WELL AND THEN SOME ... NO MATTER WHAT!®

As I continued my worldwide tour to various places proclaiming the miraculous healing that God had given me, I began to be overwhelmed with an abundance of "GRATITUDE"!

In December 2001, my workplace, which is the Conway Human Development Center in Conway, AR, began to experience a severe budget crisis and several long and short term employees were laid off. I work in staff training and no one was being hired for me to train. Rather that laying me off, a decision was made to float me to the kitchen to help the staff there. I elected to help on the "pot sink" washing pots and pans. I was very grateful to still have a job to go to everyday, and it really didn't matter where they sent me. Each day that I would enter the kitchen I would tell the staff, who were overworked and feeling down, to PUT SOME GRATITUDE IN YOUR ATTITUDE!® They soon grew weary of my continued recitation of that statement, but I didn't give up on trying to encourage them to be grateful and thankful that we still had a job! Sometime they would hate to see me coming because they knew what I was going to tell them. Over a period of time after they saw that I was not going to quit telling them that, they began to tell others to PUT SOME GRATITUDE IN YOUR ATTITUDE!® It soon became my number one slogan and in 2003 I applied for and received a registered trademark on it!

The slogan PUT SOME GRATITUDE IN YOUR ATTITUDE!® has become so infectious and contagious all over the country and throughout the world until I was impressed by God to use it as the title of this book!

15

Too often we complain about what we don't have, rather than being thankful and grateful for what we have. As I reflected back over the illness that I had and my consistent "ALL IS WELL" faith in God, even in the midst of the storm, I suddenly realized that God had given me the strength and courage to "PUT SOME GRATITUDE IN MY ATTITUDE". I didn't complain about my condition, but I just told Him, "Thank you, LORD"! I realize that it's not over until God says it's over!

All of us will have some storms of some sort to blow into our lives, but we don't have to allow them to consume us. With God's help we can make it through whatever storm we may face and rather than becoming bitter, we can choose to become better! This is what God did for me! I became better after having gone through the storm than I was before I entered it.

I pray that this book will be a source of encouragement to you as you read it, regardless and irrespective of what your storm may be. All storms are not of the same magnitude and intensity, but we can always count on God to be right by our side through every one of them as He has been for me all the days of my life. Everyday was not always easy for me, but I continued to say "ALL IS WELL"! I experienced some of the most difficult days that I had ever had in my life, but God was there for me and He will be there for you too! I had to stand on God's word in spite of how things looked and regardless of what the doctor's were telling me! As you read this book and as you share it with others, I pray that in the midst of it all, that God will give you the strength, the courage, the faith and the perseverance to PUT SOME GRATITUDE IN YOUR ATTITUDE!®

FOREWORD I
Marie Johnson

I didn't really know the real danger that my husband faced concerning the medication he was on during his illness. He wouldn't tell me for fear that I couldn't deal with it along with all the other responsibilities I had placed on me. I was really upset when I found this out but I realized that he only did it because he loved me so.

"I will bless the Lord at all times: his praise shall continually be in my mouth. My soul shall make her boast in the Lord: the humble shall hear thereof, and be glad. O magnify the Lord with me, and let us exalt his name together." **Psalms 34:1-3**

I have heard this scripture read many, many times and also quoted it many times. But until my husband became ill I realized that I never really knew the true meaning of it. There will come a time in all of our lives when we will be tested by the word of God. This is the time when we will truly find out if God's word lives within us. My husband proved that God's word is true and alive and that the devil is a liar twenty-four hours a day.

I have truly been touched and inspired by the way my husband handled his illness with the help of God. God's word said "Why die when you can live?" My husband chose to live to tell the world about the healing power of our Great God. I admire him for the stand he took against all the odds in his sickness. He knew beyond a shadow of doubt that his God was able. God blessed him to "PUT SOME GRATITUDE IN HIS ATTITUDE!" I am sure that after reading this book you will be persuaded to PUT SOME GRATITUDE IN YOUR ATTITUDE!®

So many people were touched by his attitude toward his illness and his love for God even at the door of death. I will be the first to admit that things got pretty frustrating for me, and at times I felt as if I couldn't handle it anymore. But each time I came into his hospital room to visit I was encouraged through his faith in God to continue on and not give up. Through my husband's illness I have become a stronger person. The saying, "I would rather see a sermon than hear one," became reality for me during this time.

I thank God for His love and for His word that is everlasting. Since God has brought us through my husband's illness and recovery, we have become closer and more understanding of each other's feelings.

Always remember that God never makes mistakes and He is a God that will never leave you nor forsake you. All you have to do is trust Him and take Him at his word and, most of all, take the limits off God. If there is someone going through a crisis now, God is your only hope. Trust him. He will bring you through! Roy, I love you and always will. I will always be there for you and of course, "ALL IS WELL."

Romans 8:28- And we Know that all things work together for good to them that love God, to them who are the called according to his purpose." So many good things have come out of the illness of my husband, and I know many more good things are still to come.

GOD BLESS YOU! I LOVE YOU SO MUCH!

Your wife,

Marie Johnson
Little Rock, Arkansas

FOREWORD II
Charles Johnson

Roy Johnson is my brother in the faith, my brother in the spirit, and my brother in the flesh. He is and has always been my multi-dimensional brother. Actually, books could be written about each dimension of my brotherhood.

My first memory of Roy was one warm August day in 1950. I have a vivid memory of all of the male children of the Johnson household being hustled out of the home by at least three or four women all dressed in white and being sent to Mrs. Brice's house to play with our good friends, Authur and Willie H.

I took the liberty to ask one of the ladies at the risk of being told to "Mind your own business," what was going on, she then took the time to talk with me before telling me to, "Run along," that I was about to get a brand new little brother or sister from the Lord. Feeling that we should not be anywhere close when the Lord got there, we took off. I later learned that the lady that I spoke with was a very famous southern midwife who had delivered many babies in Stuttgart and surrounding towns in Arkansas.

Roy was born at a time when there were not many hospitals for a black child to be born in, and my mother had no choice but to give birth at our home. Later that day we were allowed to return home and all of the ladies in white were praising the Lord for a healthy baby boy. Finally, we were escorted into my mother's bedroom to say hello to my new brother, who was only hours old.

He is my brother in faith because during his near death illness, from his hospital bed he was one of faith's most outspoken prophets. No matter how sick he was, instead of allowing people to speak words of comfort to him, he took on the role of speaking words of comfort to them. On the telephone his personality was so upbeat, many would ask, "Why is he in there?" while the doctors on his medical team who saw him on a daily basis would ask, "What is keeping him alive?"

Roy decided to keep his eyes on his God rather than on his circumstances. In his now famous trademark statement, ALL IS WELL AND THEN SOME...NO MATTER WHAT!® Roy in a biblical sense, decided to call those things that were not as though they were. He decided that his best course of action was to speak life over what some had concluded would be impending doom.

Through the eyes of faith, he saw in the spirit what was impossible for others to see looking through the physical. Through the eyes of faith, he literally saw an amazing grace which supplied him with a well of optimism that gave him all of the hope he needed to keep the faith, while in the physical realm, hope was fading fast. Like Job, Roy Johnson decided to wait upon the Lord. Like Job, the Lord came and healed him. Like Job, the Lord is giving him double for his trouble.

After reading this book I am convinced that you will be inspired to PUT SOME GRATITUDE IN YOUR ATTITUDE!®

Charles Johnson
Detroit, Michigan

A REPORT FROM
MY RHEUMATOLOGIST
Dr. Christopher D. Adams

Roy Johnson first came into my office on December 30, 1994. Like many patients I see as an arthritis and connective tissue disease expert, he entered my examination room pushed by his wife in a wheelchair. Unlike my other patients, he was a young man without the obvious deformities I usually see in arthritic conditions such as rheumatoid arthritis. Roy was so weak that he could barely extend his arm for a handshake. In fact, he raised his wrist up off of the armrest of the wheelchair because he was unable to pull his elbow up due to weakness in his shoulder muscles. His head sagged forward on his chest. I will never forget how he cocked his head gently to the side and smiled as he told me "doc, I have been a little weak recently." We reviewed his medical history. Earlier that summer he had begun to feel tired. He had gradual progression of weakness which involved virtually his entire body. He had trouble coughing and even swallowing. He had a very thorough evaluation by his internal medicine specialist to exclude the possibility of cardiac problems. He also had a very complete neurological evaluation by his neurologist to make sure he had no neurological illness. His internist was concerned because a recent chemistry test had returned abnormal. His creatinine phosphokinase (CPK) was an astounding 30,000 mg/dl. Normally, there is only about 300 mg/dl in the blood stream. As my evaluation progressed, it became very apparent that Mr. Johnson had a condition known as dermatomyositis. This is a poorly understood medical condition in which the body's own immune system begins attacking the muscles and skin. Dermatomyositis is a rare disease that causes profound weakness in all of the muscles of the body. Not only are the voluntary muscles involved, but sometimes even the involuntary muscles are affected. In other words, a patient may have difficulty moving his arms and legs as well as trouble swallowing or even difficulty breathing. Sometimes the muscles in the throat and chest get so weak that patients will choke on their own saliva. Occasionally the chest muscles get so weak that ventilator support and artificial respiration is required. While some patients have a relatively mild case, other patients can have a progressive and inexorable downhill course leading to eventual death. The treatment of severe dermatomyositis is difficult. It involves very strong medication with potentially severe side effects. The illness can smolder for years, or can suddenly flare up to create life threatening consequences within only a few days. Nobody knows what causes dermatomyositis. Although we can treat the illness and its complications, doctors don't usually speak of a "cure" when they discuss its treatment. Roy's case was certainly one of the worst I had ever seen. He and I discussed the serious implications of this illness. We discussed measures which might be helpful to treat him. I emphasized that cures were not unheard of, but were uncommon. I broached the issue of hospitalization for treatment. He wasn't enthusiastic about coming into the hospital, but said he would do it if that is what needed to be done.

Like all clinicians, I occasionally play hunches. As a spiritual man, I jokingly tell my patients that I depend upon the "divine inspirations". Something in the back of my head told me that Roy was too sick to be treated at home. I walked down the hallway to discuss his illness with a rheumatologic colleague of mine. The two of us agreed that his case was tenuous and that he could be best treated in the hospital. I returned to tell Roy and his wife that both my colleague and I felt he needed hospitalization. That turned out to be a very good choice. He was admitted the afternoon of December 30th, 1994. He was hospitalized until February 2nd, 1995.

During his hospitalization he initially got worse. The muscle inflammation was so severe that he experienced a condition called rhabdomyolysis. This is a fancy Greek word that basically means "melting away of the muscles". The inflammation was so intense that his muscles were actually being destroyed. In addition to intravenous steroid medicine, we gave him therapy with

22

intravenous gammaglobulin. The combination of these medicines made his blood pressure go up to unacceptably high levels, so we had to ask a kidney specialist to assist with his care. He remained too weak to get out of bed by himself. He had a muscle biopsy done on January 12, 1995. The pathologist felt very secure in his diagnosis of a "classic case of dermatomyositis".

Gradually Roy had less difficulty breathing. He had less difficulty swallowing. Nevertheless, he seemed to be making very slow progress. The second week of his hospitalization we again gave him very high doses of intravenous steroids and gave him another course of intravenous gammaglobulin. I was so concerned by his lack of progress that I even had the pathologist review results of his muscle biopsy. The pathologist seemed mildly offended as if I were questioning his expertise. I told him that I simply had to double check all my facts and figures, since Roy wasn't getting better as fast as I wanted. Despite the high steroid dose he was receiving and his other medicines, I was worried about his recovery.

During his hospitalization, Roy was an inspiration and wonderfully positive motivator for the nurses in the hospital. Despite his very serious illness, his spirits were unflagging. Roy knew where his source of strength lay, and I am firmly convinced that his faith had a lot to do with his improvement. Finally, by the 2nd of February, he was able to get out of bed and stand up on his own. He still couldn't raise his arms above shoulder level and he still couldn't walk more than the distance from his bed to the bathroom in his hospital room. We started a medication called Methotrexate. Methotrexate is ordinarily used to treat cancer, but is also used in severe cases of inflammatory muscle disease, such as dermatomyositis.

When I saw him in the clinic two weeks after his hospitalization he still had to come in a wheelchair, but could push up out of the chair by himself. A month after that he was still able to move okay, but had developed diabetes as a result of his need for steroid medication. His spirits remained good. He could now hold his head up and look me in the eye as he smiled and gave me his trademark expression "all is well!" Over the next several months he made slow and gradual progress. He was able to go back to work on a part-time basis. Months turned into years and his healing progressed. He was able to discontinue his steroid medication and still did well. His blood pressure gradually became better controlled. By the spring of 1997, Roy was able to travel throughout the Southeast to proclaim his testimony. He told me he was preaching the gospel and claiming the miracle cure he had received from his dermatomyositis. He did so well that we stopped the Methotrexate therapy in April of 1997.

I have seen Roy back regularly about every three to four months since then. I am proud to proclaim that his miraculous healing has resulted in a remission from his dermatomyositis. From a medical standpoint, he is now as fit as if he had never experienced this serious illness.

I tell my patients that miracles occur. When they become hopeless and helpless because of their chronic problems, I remind them that I have personally witnessed divine intervention and physical healing at the hands of Providence. When I tell my patients this, I often think of my good friend Roy Johnson. I recall how his spirit was never "sick" even when he had a hard time breathing because of his muscle weakness. I recall how his attitude remained upbeat even when he had a difficult time swallowing water. I know that I have seen a physical healing in Mr. Johnson that can only be described as a miracle. I consider myself lucky to count Roy Johnson as a personal friend.

CHRISTOPHER D. ADAMS, M.D., F.A.C.P
June 16th, 1998

COMMENTS FROM MY SUPERVISOR

Ed Jennings

When I was transferred into the role of Staff Development Coordinator at the Conway Human Development Center in the early 1980's, I was also facing some staff additions. By the position being in Staff Development, it brought many inquiries and applicants for the vacant position. Not recalling the specific dates or circumstances, I remember thinking about my brief acquaintance and times that I was around a man named Roy Johnson. Roy was working in the Little Rock area, and he and I crossed paths enough times that I was able to determine something very special about him. I do not recall if I contacted him or not but I do recall his application and interview. I was immediately convinced that Roy was my "overwhelming" choice to fill one of the vacant positions. I submitted his name to my supervisor, Mr. Bob Clark, who also knew Roy and he immediately approved the request. That was the beginning of our employee/supervisor relationship. It has been 17 years of the most pleasant employee/employer relationships that I have ever experienced. Prior to being transferred to Staff Development, I had worked as Director of Education, supervising up to 120 teachers and paraprofessionals. This experience was over a 15-year period. Although I had many outstanding individuals working for me, Roy is one of the finest employees that I have ever supervised. He is not only my great friend but more importantly, my brother in Christ.

It is difficult for me to put in words how I might describe Roy. To put it briefly but emphatically, he is the most Christ like; others centered individual that I have ever known. He is a living example of what a true Christian ought to be. He is not only an outstanding person but is an excellent role model and trainer for staff. He has a magnetic personality. One of his favorite expressions is "Attitudes are Contagious". I pray for an epidemic of

Roy Johnson's positive attitude that extends throughout the Conway Human Development Center. One example that is immediately seen in Roy with new staff is his ability to remember names. We have now and have had for a number of years, approximately 1250 employees. I really believe that you could line them up and Roy could name 95% of them, first and last name. The amazing thing about this is his short association with the great majority of them while in class. Roy is also able to be a witness through his never ending smile and his "All is Well" constant attitude. Only God knows the impact that he has and continues to have on the entire staff at CHDC. Many people have come to know Jesus Christ as a result of Roy's testimony and personal witness.

The first 15 years of Roy's employment with the Conway Human Development Center was smooth sailing and certainly "All was Well". One morning during the summer of 1994 an employee came in my office and said Roy had fallen in the parking lot. Having never heard a complaint from Roy about not feeling well or anything physically bothering him, I assumed that he had tripped or something of that nature. As I recall, that was the first indicator of a physical problem that would develop into a life-threatening condition. Over the next few months Roy's condition got worse but still without complaint. His constant, contagious smile was always there. He missed work occasionally because of not feeling well but while here he never refused an assignment and continued to do his work. Roy, not being one to talk about anything negative, refused to admit or accept his limitations until his condition forced him to. We noticed a slowing down, perhaps some slurred speech, and a few other physical changes taking place. As he started seeing different doctors, we became more and more concerned about him. One of the most difficult things for any of us is to experience physical problems of an unknown nature that cannot be diagnosed. Being privileged to work with many other Christian people, we began to pray for Roy as we became more and more concerned. His welfare was our number one prayer issue in the department. He never seemed to object to our many questions, such as, "Roy, it might be this or that", or Why don't you go to another specialist? This went on for days and weeks and finally the Christmas vacation of 1994 came around. We literally had to walk Roy to his car so that he could try to drive home and we insisted that he "get something done". Through a series of test he was finally diagnosed with a life-threatening muscle disease called dermatomyositis and was immediately hospitalized. We first heard all kinds of stories about his condition and we became more concerned about the unknown.

During the coming weeks of his hospitalization, which began on December 30, 1994 and ended on February 2, 1995, we were in daily contact with him by phone and many of us visited him regularly. He was off from work until May, 1995. The nurses, doctors, and support staff at St. Vincent's soon came to know and love Roy Johnson the way we do. They could not believe the number of calls, letters, cards, flowers, gifts, and other gestures of love that he received. He had the same effect on them that he has on all of us. He probably is one of a few patients that nurses would fight over who got to take care of him. He, although near death, maintained his trust in God and faith that "All Is Well". His smile was never erased and his love for the hospital staff was apparent.

Following his time in the hospital and recovery period, I was wondering how we would make it at work without him. Still dealing with many fears and the "unknown" I was trying to decide, could anybody fill in for Roy during his absence? Obviously, no one could fill his shoes, but we managed to adjust schedules and survive. I remember telling Roy as he lay there helpless, that God was allowing him to be on the other end of giving. We so enjoyed giving back to Roy, a small portion of what he had given us. It was obviously difficult, at first, for Roy not to be the one giving, sharing, caring and loving. His life, his illness and everything about him has taught us all so much.

Roy is a shining example of the scripture that reminds us to be thankful in all things, for this is the will of God. God has so used this man and continues to do so in bringing hope to all of us.

He has now extended his "All Is Well" to include "ALL IS WELL AND THEN SOME"! I am personally so blessed to have him for a very special brother, employee and friend. God blessed us and hundreds of other friends and families, when He decided that Roy's work here on earth is not yet completed. Thank God for the few Roy Johnson's in this world! "ALL IS WELL AND THEN SOME"!

Today, some 3 years later, he is doing great, giving God all of the glory and credit for his healing. Do I believe in miracles? I do and always have. I thank God that he chooses, under his sovereign plan, to show us His healing power through special people like Roy.

Proverbs 25:13, (Living Bible) A faithful employee is as refreshing as a cool day in the hot summer time.

Roy certainly is a messenger who is faithful in his work and diligent in his efforts to serve others.

ED JENNINGS
STAFF DEVELOPMENT SUPERVISOR
CONWAY HUMAN DEVELOPMENT CENTER
CONWAY, ARKANSAS (1998)

COMMENTS FROM
A CO-WORKER
Jackie Brigance

Around August of 1994, Roy came by the office to say hello to the staff. He seemed to be very exhausted. He was sweating and made the statement that he was tired. One of the secretaries asked him, "Are you hot?" He replied, "Yes, I am." He went on to say that he was having some problems with his shoulder and arms. We teased him that shaking so many hands could be the problem. He said he wondered if that was it himself.

Over the next few months when I visited with Brother Roy in his office, I could see that his condition worsened tremendously over a period of three months. On several occasions I would stop by his office to check on him and he would make the statement that his legs were giving out on him. He mentioned that they seemed numb at times and that there seemed to be poor circulation to his legs. I would go by and he would be exercising his legs, lifting them up, down and around off of the floor. Once I asked him why was he moving his legs and feet like that and he replied, "My circulation seems to be poor and I exercise them to keep them from getting numb, but "ALL IS WELL!"

The worst that I ever saw him was in December 1994 when I went by his office to check on him. As I entered the door I overheard several employees saying Roy wasn't himself and that he was staying in his office and was barely walking. As I went to enter his office one employee stopped me and shared with me the condition he was in the day before. She said, "Yesterday, Roy Johnson was so weak he could barely walk. We were concerned about him driving himself home and offered to take him home or call his wife, but he said, "I'll make it, I'll be okay, ALL IS WELL." They told me that they called his wife to look out for him just in case he didn't make it home. The two ladies were Mary Holloway, one of the switchboard operators, and her daughter, Shelly McNeil.

I went to his office, surprised that he was even at work after hearing the condition that he was in the day before. I said, "Roy, how are you doing?" He replied, "ALL IS WELL." One thing that I can say is that through all of the pain and suffering that he experienced, he still greeted you with, "ALL IS WELL." A strong willed and determined person is Roy Johnson. I went on to tell him about what I had heard about his condition the day before. He said, "Yes, it's true, I could barely walk and I had difficulty driving, but I made it home." When he got there he said his wife and children were standing in the door waiting and looking for him to drive up. He said he made it home with only a few minor problems. We went on to discuss that his doctors had not been able to find out what was wrong with him or why he is losing strength in his arms, hands, legs and feet. He said that the doctors were still running tests to find out what is wrong with him. It is strange that while we were talking Roy's phone rang and it rang again. Well, in my mind I was thinking, I wonder if he can answer the phone but I didn't want to offend him or make him feel helpless so I finally asked if he would like for me to answer his phone for him. He said, "Yes, would you please." I did and he talked with the person and once he finished, he handed me the phone, and I hung it up for him. At that moment, I knew that this man was very, very ill.

I went on to ask him how did he get to work today? He said, "I drove." I said, "You drove? How did you drive from Little Rock to Conway?" He said, "The Good Lord saw to me getting here."

He said that he was so weak he didn't know how he did it himself. He could not even stretch his arm out to reach the phone when it rang. He was so right when he said the Lord saw to him getting to work on that day. He went on to explain how he drove up and down the highway that week. He said that he drove with one foot on the gas and had to pick up his other leg and put it on the brake pedal whenever he got ready to stop. He said that his reflexes were slow, so he had to think about what he would need to do in order to operate his vehicle long before he actually needed to do it. He said that he was a better driver then than he had ever been in his life. I was shocked. He is a fighter! I never heard Roy say, "I give up." I am sure that there were many days, especially during this time, that he could have said it but not once did I hear him say it. I did hear him say that regardless of how much pain and suffering that he was going through, that "ALL IS WELL" or "It will get better." I thank God that all turned out well for him.

Roy, you are one of the greatest! You are strong, you are determined, you are a fighter, and you are a very caring person! Thanks for showing me that faith is the way.

Jackie Brigance
Conway Human Development Center
Conway, Arkansas (1998)

BEFORE ENTERING
THE HOSPITAL
May 1, 1994 - December 30, 1994

Around May 1, 1994, I started experiencing severe pain in both of my arms. I found it very difficult to work or to sleep at night. I had to sleep with one arm hanging off the side of the bed to get some relief. I endured the pain for several weeks, thinking that it would eventually all go away. Pain medication helped some but the excruciating pain would soon return.

Since nothing was helping, I sought medical attention at St. Vincent Medical Center emergency room on Wednesday, June 29, 1994 after I got home from work. I told my wife that I was going to get the pain in my arms checked out and that I should be back home as soon as I possibly could. I was examined by the emergency room physician and he detected an abnormal EKG, which really was normal for me. They immediately assumed that the pain in both arms was probably related to possible problems with my heart. My family doctor was in the hospital recuperating from major surgery and could not be reached to inform the emergency room doctors that the EKG was normal for me. About 10:00 P.M. that night, I telephoned my wife to tell her that they had examined me and that I should be coming home soon. I did this not knowing at the time that the doctors were planning to keep me. By the time that I had gotten dressed, I was advised that they would need to keep me overnight for observation. I was shocked and bewildered because I had planned to go get checked out, get a prescription and return back home. I then phoned my wife and told her that I would be spending the night at the hospital for observation to determine whether the severe pain that I had been experiencing was related in any way to my abnormal EKG. Heart Specialist Dr. Joe Hargrove happened to have been in the emergency room area that night and I asked them to call him in so that I could consult with him. He answered many, many questions for me, and he told me that he felt like it was a good idea for me to go ahead and spend the night in spite of my desire to go home. He told me of the possible things that could happen if I left, if my heart was the problem. I was convinced that it would be wise to stay overnight for observations. I was transferred from the emergency room to room 2206 for the night.

Since I had not been a patient in a hospital in 30 years, I was greatly concerned about what may happen to me in there. By the way, I did drive myself to the hospital and my car was parked outside.

They gave me a change of clothes. After I changed into hospital clothes I left my pants on the bed with me, with my car keys in the pocket. The nurse came in, picked up my pants and proceeded to carry them across the room to the closet. I very politely asked for my pants back. I told her that I wanted to keep them on my bed so they can be close to me just in case I decided to leave the hospital during the night and go home to my wife and children. She obliged but smiled and looked cautiously at me. I really was not sure what to expect. I felt that if something was done that I disagreed with or that I thought inappropriate, I knew that I could always unplug the heart monitor that I was hooked up to and remove all of the wires, get dressed and drive myself home. I got very little or no sleep that night. I found things to do to keep me up so that the night would pass faster.

Thursday morning, June 30 finally came and I was discharged from the hospital to Dr. Joe Hargrove's office where I spent the day undergoing a series of heart evaluations and a stress test. At the end of the day I was given a clean bill of health on my heart. Praise God for that! They gave me some medication that they thought might help the pain in my arms but suggested that I should continue to seek medical attention to determine the cause of the pain in my arms. I tried the medication but I kept experiencing severe pain in both arms. Pain so severe that my sleep was frequently interrupted during the night and when morning came I felt like I had not been to bed at all.

33

I kept praying and asking God for direction. The Bible, in **Proverbs 3:5-6,** says:

(5) "Trust in the Lord with all thine heart; and lean not unto thine own understanding". (6) "In all thy ways acknowledge him and he shall direct thy paths".

I then began to consult other doctors about the pain that I was having in my arms. Not long after the pain in my arms I began to experience rashes on my chest, face, hands and fingers. My hands became discolored and swollen and cuts would come on my fingers for seemingly no reason. I would keep them bandaged up a lot, which got me a lot of attention at work. Many people would ask me, "What happened to your poor little fingers?" I would smile and say, "ALL IS WELL," because I had put it all in the hands of God and whatever the problem was, I knew that he could handle it. After awhile my condition began to worsen and it became more obvious to my family and me that something was terribly wrong. I remember on one occasion I was asked by my family to open the top on a mayonnaise jar. I attempted to open it but the muscles in my hand had gotten so weak that I did not have enough strength to open it. I tried to make a game out of it with my 17 year old son to see if he was strong enough to open it but it didn't work and it continued to become more obvious that I was a very sick man. However, I still said, "ALL IS WELL," not all is perfect, but "ALL IS WELL." That quote was given to me by Judy Chappell, a friend and co-worker. The other part of that is, Today is the tomorrow that worried you yesterday and ALL IS WELL! Another quote that I have in my office is, "Lord remind me that nothing will happen to me today that you and I together can't handle. My son commented one day, "Daddy, you are really getting feeble." He was very right, but I smiled and went on my way trusting that God would intervene and make everything all right.

As time progressed I continued to see various doctors. One thought that I might have carpal tunnel syndrome, which could cause weakness in the hands. It got so that I could not close my

34

hands up. Carpal Tunnel Syndrome was ruled out as a possible cause for my illness. I continued to go to other doctors and specialists for evaluations. By this time it is November, 1994 and no specific cause for my illness has been determined. I am still holding on to my faith in God because I know that He will see me through whatever the reason is for my sudden illness. I was deteriorating daily but I continued to drive to work at the Conway Human Development Center in Conway, AR. This is about 45 minutes from my home in Little Rock.

Everyone who was aware of my condition was so kind, compassionate, and understanding towards me. My family, my friends, my co-workers, my fellow church members, the individuals who live where I work and everyone has made this very puzzling situation much easier to deal with. My supervisor Mr. Ed Jennings, all of my co-workers in staff development, dietetics, the Superintendent of the Human Development center, Mr. Bob Clark, his assistant Ms. Carol Shockley and their staff, the personnel director Carolyn Coney and her staff, and the entire staff and clients of the Human Development center have been exceptionally kind and helpful to me.

My church family, the Williams Temple Church of God In Christ, Little Rock, AR, and Pastor Jewel Withers Jr. have been outstanding in showing their love and concern for me. Other churches and friends in and out of the city of Little Rock have rallied to the cause. With all of the love and concern that people are showing me, no matter what happens to me, "ALL IS WELL!"

As time progressed I began to notice that I was having difficulty in walking and climbing steps. On Sunday November 20, 1994, while at church I noticed a severe weakness in my right leg while entering the pulpit. When I began to elevate it to go up into the pulpit, it went limp. In an effort for it not to seem obvious that something was wrong with me, I went ahead and forced my leg up in order to enter the pulpit. At this time I was convinced more than ever that I was a very sick man, as other areas of my body in addition to my arms and hands began to be severely affected. I also began to have difficulties with eating and swallowing.

35

By this time with my arms and hands and skin rash I had consulted with a cardiologist, an orthopedic physician and a dermatologist.

After my legs became weak it was not long before my back muscles became weak. Soon after that the muscles in my neck became very weak and it not only became very difficult for me to walk, but it became very difficult for me to stand for any length of time. As time moved on the muscles in my neck continued to deteriorate and it became very difficult for me to hold my head up.

Our family during the entire year of 1994 was dealing with the severe illness of my wife's mother, Mrs. Lillie Pearl Page. We traveled back and forth most of the year to visit her in hospitals in Texarkana, Hope, Prescott and Hot Springs, AR. Many times my wife would have to drive because of the increasing physical problems that I was experiencing. My mother-in-law passed away on Tuesday, November 29, 1994 around 8:15 A.M. at National Park Medical Center in Hot Springs, AR, with my wife at her bedside. She had gone to visit her on Monday, November 28 and felt impressed to spend the night with her and she passed away before she left on Tuesday morning. My wife is to be highly commended for her diligent effort in taking care of me and also dealing with the stress of her mother's illness and her passing away. It appeared that my condition may have been heading in the same direction, but "ALL IS WELL."

Each day I was becoming weaker and weaker. On Wednesday, November 30, I consulted with Neurosurgeon Dr. Robert Abraham, because I thought that maybe something was happening in my brain to cause the problems that I was experiencing. Dr. Abraham examined me and was very disturbed at the severe weakness that he observed. I was barely able to walk. His initial feeling was that I had a pinched nerve in my back. He sent me immediately to Southwest Hospital for an MRI of my lower back and neck. During this time I could hear the popping of cerebral fluid every time that I moved my neck. The results of the MRI indicated that there was nothing wrong with my back or neck. My condition continued to deteriorate moment by moment, hour by hour, and day by day.

During this time we were making funeral arrangements for my wife's mother. The funeral was held on Saturday, December 3, 1994, in Willisville, AR. Many people, including my mother, were not fully aware of the extent of my illness. I did get to attend the funeral but I could barely walk and I was in excruciating pain. My wife had always been there for me, and I felt that I had to be there for her on the day of her mother's funeral. I nearly blacked out several times because of the stress and strain of the day's activities and this is the first time that I have shared this with anyone. No one but God and me knows the extent of the pain and suffering that I was experiencing. My outward appearance and my physical condition were both perishing, but my inward and spiritual conditions were flourishing. I petitioned God that whatever you do and whatever you allow to be taken away from me, "just do not take your spirit away from me." I know that I can weather any storm with God's spirit dwelling within me.

I continued to go to work and to drive, although I was very weak. My legs became so weak that it made it very difficult for me to get around, but I kept on saying, "ALL IS WELL," because again I knew that God was in control and that "circumstances do not make a man they just reveal what he is made of". People did not and many do not understand when I say , "ALL IS WELL" , but I am going to keep saying it because I know that whatever happens to me God knows all about it and whatever He allows to happen to me is not to make me bitter but to make me better!

Therefore, I continued to say, "ALL IS WELL," even when I needed help in getting in and out of the car. I became a much better driver during this time because I became more cautious. I knew that my reflexes were slower, so I anticipated that things would occur long before they actually did and I would take my hand, which was very weak to pick up my leg and put it on and off of the brake pedal. It took me two hours or more to get dressed for work each morning. My wife and children would often help me do the things that I could not do. I kept driving and I kept going to work.

Sometimes I had to stop and hold on to someone or something in order to make it to the building. Once I would make it to my office that is where I would be for the next 8 hours, unless I had a class to teach. During this time I got my doctor to complete a form for me to get a temporary handicapped parking sticker so I could park close to the building. The lady at the Revenue office looked at me, observed my severe physical condition, and asked if I would like to apply for a permanent handicap license plate. I smiled and thanked her for her concern but I assured her that this would only be a temporary condition. As much as I love to go out on campus at work, to greet, and shake hands with staff and clients, I got to where I could no longer do that. I just was not physically able to walk out on the grounds anymore.

Many of my fellow employees, friends, and clients, realizing that my physical condition was fastly deteriorating, came to visit me in my office.

At this time I am under the care of Internal Medicine Specialist, Dr. Raymond Miller, who was diligently evaluating my condition and trying to determine what was causing the weakness in my body. I advised him that I thought that I needed to be admitted to the hospital. He told me that they were running the same test outside of the hospital that they would be running if I were in there and all I would be doing is running up a big hospital bill without them knowing what to treat me for. I very reluctantly accepted this train of thought, although I did not necessarily agree with it. Fellow employees and family could not understand it either, although I tried unsuccessfully to let them know that in spite of it all, "ALL IS WELL." I did finally understand it though, after spending 35 days in the hospital and realizing that my hospital bill and doctor bills had gone over the $100,000 mark and they knew what was wrong with me, but "ALL IS WELL."

Employees who visited me in my office quickly recognized the fact that I was a very sick man and that they felt that I should not be at work. I told them that since I did not know what was wrong with me and neither did the doctors know, I felt that I should continue to come to work so that if I had to go in the hospital I would still have some sick time. Dr. Raymond Miller was wonderful! Each time that he would get a test result back that would rule out a specific condition, he would call me at work and let me know. This was very reassuring to know that my doctor cared enough to keep in constant contact with me.

There were times when friends would come by my office to check on me and while they were there they would have to answer my telephone for me when it would ring because I was not physically able to extend my arms far enough to reach it.

On Friday, December 16, 1994, I stayed at home alone, because of being too weak to go to work. As I was lying on the couch in the living room the phone rang. When I tried to get up to answer it I realized that my muscles were too weak to get up. The phone was steadily ringing and I was still on the couch. I frantically tried to muster up enough strength to get up, but continued to fall. At this point I decided that I would try to roll off of the couch and onto the floor. I was successful at this, but the phone continued to ring. I am thinking that it is probably my wife calling to check on me, and she thinks something probably has happened to me. If it was her, and if she did think that, she was absolutely right. Something had happened. The phone suddenly stopped after ringing about 25 times. I am still on the floor in the living room unable to get on my feet. I began to drag myself on the floor to the kitchen. While on my way the phone begins to ring again, another 25 times. By this time I was in the kitchen trying to pull up on something so I could try to extend my arm to the phone, which is on the wall. By the time that I was able to pull the cord down and grab the receiver, it stopped ringing. I thought that I may have had a stroke and that maybe this was the reason I could not walk. This had never happened to me before. I became very concerned and I called my wife to see if she had been trying to reach me.

She said it was not her. I told her that I felt that she needed to come home from work to check on me because I had gotten where I could no longer walk. In the meantime I was able to pull up on a chair high enough to raise the kitchen window in case I needed to call 911 for help. At least they would be able to get to me. The front door was locked as well as the screen door. My wife immediately left work to come home to see about me. When she arrived I had regained enough strength to go to the front door and unlock the screen so she could get in.

I was feeling some better by the time that she arrived, and within a few hours I was able to regain some use of my legs. God truly blessed me through the whole ordeal. The next day I purchased a portable phone so that I would not have to get up to answer it.

I found out later that some employees from work had tried to call me during the time when I was not able to get to the phone. This was the day of our annual Christmas potluck sponsored by the employees in the housekeeping department. I had assisted them in putting this together and had attended it for the last 12 years. This year I was too sick and too weak to make it. As a gesture of their concern for me, they had set up a speaker phone in the area of the dinner so that every one in attendance could say hello to me and sing some Christmas carols to me over the phone. I told them later that the 50 times that they let the phone ring, I was struggling trying to get to it to answer it. I was so sorry that I missed out on the great opportunity to hear from them. I graciously thanked them later for their kind expression of love. My health continued to decline after that, but I continued to go to work. God gave me strength enough to go back to work for a few more days after that incident.

I continued to work up until December 22, 1994, 8 days before I went in the hospital. The reason I did not continue to go to work was because of the approaching Christmas holidays. I knew that I was going down fast, and I knew the Christmas holidays were fastly approaching. I decided that I had better go to Wal-Mart to do some Christmas shopping for my family. I was able to make it in the store and get the motorized cart for the disabled and I drove around the store and got a few items and made it back home and "ALL IS WELL."

Before leaving work on Thursday, December 22nd, I had a feeling that it would be awhile before I would return. It was three days before Christmas. At this point I am in a very weakened and deteriorated condition. My hands, my feet and my legs are very, very weak and severely swollen. I am barely getting around. I have lost most of the use of my arms, hands and legs. I am very, very weak. I stayed at work late today to try to straighten up my office some before I left for the Christmas holidays. I don't know when I will be able to return. It is now around 5:00 P.M. I think I have done enough. I am very weak and exhausted. My condition is deteriorating daily. My doctors are still running tests to try to find out what is wrong with me, but they haven't come up with anything yet. I feel that they are doing everything that they can. I will have to be patient. I know God has not forgotten about me. A co-worker of mine, Kaye Malcom, deliberately stayed late today because she knew that I didn't need to be left alone.

It is now about 5:15 P.M. Kaye and I prepare to leave the office. As I attempted to lock the office door, I realized that I could not elevate my arm and hand to the level of the lock. Kaye compassionately tells me that she will lock it for me. I graciously thanked her, and, in spite of my condition, I told her that "ALL IS WELL!" She observed me in the worst physical condition that I had been in to this point. She asked me if I would like for her to drive me home to Little Rock. I work in Conway, which is about 30 miles from Little Rock. I thanked her but told her that I felt as if I could make it okay. Again I told her that "ALL IS WELL". Kaye very reluctantly accepted my decision to drive home alone but she alerted Mary Holloway, the switchboard operator who was on duty, and her daughter Shellie McNeil, of my deteriorated condition. Mary and Shellie tried unsuccessfully to convince me to allow one of them to drive me home, but again I graciously thanked them and told them that I felt I could make it. Shellie tearfully asked me if I would allow her to help me to my car, since I was determined to drive myself home. I consented and she helped me get in the car. I thanked her for her kindness and, I began my journey to Little Rock, very confident that God would give me the strength to make it, regardless of my feeble condition. Shellie, however, returned to the switchboard and told her mother that she had major concerns about me making it home safely. Mary immediately called my wife and told her that I was on my way home and that it would probably be a good idea to go out and look for me if I didn't make it home within a reasonable period of time. As I pulled up in the driveway in a very weakened condition, I observed my wife, my daughter, and my son standing in the front door watching the vehicles as they approached the house, hoping that one of them would be mine. When they realized that one of them was me, they were thoroughly relieved and their hearts were filled with joy and thanksgiving to God that He had allowed me to arrive home safely. It was now around 6:25 P.M. I immediately went to the telephone and called Mary and Shellie and told them that I made it home safely and "ALL IS WELL!" They were so relieved and happy!

On Friday, December 23rd at 12 noon, I was evaluated again by my family physician, Dr. Raymond Miller. I was also seen by Dr. Miller on December 20th. He has been working diligently and faithfully to try to pinpoint what is happening to me. Each time he gets a test result back that rules out a particular illness, he calls me and lets me know. This has been very comforting to me, knowing that he is doing all he can to help me. On this day, the 23rd of December, Dr. Miller is saddened as he looked out of his window and observed the deteriorated physical condition I was in, as my wife struggled to get me out of the car and into his office. He has checked me for every conceivable condition that he feels is related to the problems that I am having, but to no avail. I requested again that he admit me to the hospital, but he advised me again that they were running all the tests outside the hospital that they would run if I were in there. He also said as he had told me before, that if I were in the hospital, all I would be doing is running up a big hospital bill and they would not be able to do anything for me because they had not been able to determine what is wrong with me. He said that I would need to have a muscle biopsy done to determine the disease that he suspects that I have. I asked him if he could set it up for tonight or this weekend. Today is Friday. He advised me that since it is the weekend, it would be very difficult to find someone to do it, since it is a procedure that is normally scheduled in advance and not done on an emergency basis. I asked him if he would still call around to see if he could find someone. He tried, but to no avail. I was very persistent but Dr. Miller was very patient and understanding about my concerns. I apologized to him for being so persistent, but I also expressed to him the dilemma that I was in. I knew that I was going down fast. I thanked him for trying, but told him that when I got home I would try to find someone myself to do it. Dr. Miller has been my family physician for 11 years and I think that this is the first time that he has ever questioned my sanity, but "ALL IS WELL." Since I was getting weaker and weaker daily, I wanted to make sure that everything that could be done was being done. My wife also at this time began to question my mental stability, but again "ALL IS WELL!" When I arrived home from my doctor's visit, I went straight to the telephone and made some calls to try to find a doctor that would do a muscle biopsy that night or that weekend, but needless to say, I was not successful in finding anyone. As you read this scenario, you too will probably question my sanity, but as I always say, "ALL IS WELL!"

I frequently quote an old Indian proverb that sums up the dilemma I was in: "Great Spirit grant me that I not criticize my neighbor until I have walked a mile in his moccasins."

Today is Christmas Day, December 25, 1994. The day that we celebrate the birth of our Lord and Savior Jesus Christ. My condition continues to deteriorate daily. I can't physically do the things today that I was able to do yesterday, but "ALL IS WELL!" I am physically weak but God has blessed me to be spiritually strong. God is in control and I am more than confident that whatever happens to me, "ALL IS WELL!" I am just thankful and grateful to God to still be alive!

My wife's father, Mr. Wilmer Page, and my nephew Corey Page came from Rosston, Arkansas to spend Christmas Day with us. We are still struggling with the death of my wife's mother, Mrs. Lillie Pearl Page, who passed away last month. We had a great time today, considering what we have been through. God is sustaining us. My father-in-law expresses great concern over what is happening to me. I let him know that regardless of how it looks, "ALL IS WELL." The outlook may be dark but the uplook is bright! I will continue to look up and will look to the hills from whence cometh my help. My help cometh from the Lord!

It is now Tuesday, December 27th, 1994. I have a doctor's appointment with Cardiologist Dr. Joe Hargrove at 3:00 P.M. today. I asked him to evaluate me to make sure that my heart was not a part of the reason for my problem. Dr. Hargrove is shocked to see the weakened and deteriorated condition that I am in. I have to have help getting out of my chair and onto the examination table. One of his nurses, Elaine Woods, walked in and observed my condition and her eyes began to fill up with tears because she had no idea that I was in the condition that I was in. She knew that I was sick but she didn't know that it had gotten to this point. Dr. Hargrove examined me and concluded that my heart is not the problem, but lets me know that his prayers are with me that a diagnosis will soon be made.

On Thursday, December 29, 1994, Dr. Raymond Miller, Internal Medicine Specialist, saw me in his office again and told me that he thought that he had diagnosed my case. He suspects that I have a rare muscle disease called polymyosistis. He told me that he wanted me to be evaluated by Neurologist Dr. Coburn Howell on Friday morning, December 30, 1994 at 9:00 A.M. to confirm the diagnosis.

The journal for today began about 9:00 A.M. with a visit to Neurologist Coburn Howell's office. At this point, my condition had deteriorated to its lowest level. I was a very sick man but my faith was at its highest level, "ALL WAS STILL WELL", in spite of how it looked. The visit to Dr. Howell's office was to confirm a diagnosis of polymyositis that Dr. Miller had concluded. Dr. Howell, after a thorough examination of me, also concluded that it was polymyositis, which is a rare muscle disease. The reference to the disease was later changed to dermatomyositis because along with the effect that it had on my muscles, my skin later began to develop lesions and rashes and discolorations appearing all over my body. This condition also was accompanied by severe swelling of my hands, legs and feet, with difficulty eating and swallowing.

To confirm Dr. Howell's diagnosis, he called and set up an appointment at St. Vincent Infirmary Medical Center for approximately 10:30 A.M. today to have an electromyography (EMG) done. This is a recording of electrical activity in the muscles. This test is used to diagnose diseases of the nerves and muscles. A tiny needle is inserted into a muscle. The needle was inserted several times into my legs, arms and hands. One of Dr. Howell's partners, Dr. Gordon Gibson, conducted this test.

This electromyography also confirmed the disease of dermatomyositis. Dr. Howell set up an appointment with Rheumatologist, Dr. Christopher Adams, for around 2:45 P.M. today. My wife, who had been transporting me all day, went in with me to see Dr. Adams. At this point I could no longer walk without holding on to something or somebody. My muscles were so weak, inflamed, and deteriorated I could not adequately use my hands and arms. I could no longer hold my head up. In spite of all these problems my faith in God never wavered. I still said "ALL IS WELL!"

Dr. Adams walked in, we talked, and he examined me and advised me of the possible life-threatening severity of the disease as well as the possible lifelong consequences of living with it, if I survived. He also advised me of the uncertainty of the available treatment of this rare disease and the possible consequences and side effects of being treated by the available medication. In spite of all of this, God still blessed me to hold on to the fact that "ALL IS WELL," regardless of what happens to me. Dr. Adams, being very concerned about the severity of my condition, assured me that he would hang in there with me. This was very consoling. While I was still in his office, he consulted with his fellow physicians and made calls around the country to discuss my condition with other colleagues in the medical profession. This greatly impressed me that he would go to such great lengths to try to help someone he had never met before. This showed a great deal of concern for the proper care and treatment of his new patient.

There was a great possibility that there could be heart, liver, lungs and kidney damage as a result of the medication that they would have to put me on tonight. Again, I advised him that "ALL IS WELL!" I had put it all in the hands of God!

After a very careful examination and consultation with other experts in the field, Dr. Adams concluded that time was of the essence and that I needed to be hospitalized immediately. My muscle enzyme level or (CPK) was up over 30,000 points. The normal is around 250 points or below. My muscles had shut down on me. They were very inflamed and deteriorated. Dr. Adams was very straightforward with me and told me that I was a very, very sick man. He said the prognosis did not look very good, but I said "ALL IS WELL." He advised me again that the medicine that was available to treat the disease was very potent and could cause serious heart, liver, lung, and kidney damage. Again God blessed me to respond by saying, "ALL IS WELL." Normally if there are going to be side effects they would occur within the first five days that one is on the medication. At this time I am very, very weak and fatigued. My legs, feet, and hands are severely swollen. I had to be brought to the doctor's office in a wheelchair because I was no longer able to walk alone. My physical condition was at the lowest point that it had ever been, but my spiritual condition was at the highest point that it had ever been. God gave me the necessary strength that I needed in spite of what was happening to me physically. I remembered what David said in **Psalm 121 verses 1-2:**

(1) "I will lift up mine eyes unto the hills, from whence cometh my help".(2) "My help cometh from the Lord, which made heaven and earth".

Psalm 120:1 says,

"In my distress I cried unto the Lord, and he heard me."

I also meditated on **Psalm 119:71**, when David says:

"It is good for me that I have been afflicted; that I might learn thy statutes."

All of these scriptures were of great comfort and strength to me and helped to sustain me through some of the most darkest hours of my life.

I am so glad that I had the absolute assurance that God was with me every step of the way. **Psalm 46:1** says:

"God is our refuge and strength, a very present help in trouble."

I knew that God was not allowing this to happen to me to make me bitter, but to make me better. I also realized that "no test, no testimony; no cross, no crown". God was just allowing me an opportunity to have another testimony.

Another scripture that was a great source of comfort for me was **Psalm 116, verses** 1-2, which says:

(1) "I love the Lord, because he hath heard my voice and my supplications". (2) "Because he hath inclined his ear unto me, therefore will I call upon him as long as I live."

The decision was made at about 4:15 P.M. today Friday, December 30th, 1994 to admit me to St. Vincent Infirmary Medical Center here in Little Rock, AR. I arrived at St. Vincent's at approximately 4:45 P.M. and was admitted to room 2344, 3 NW. I went straight from Dr. Adams office to the hospital. I was met by Nurse Darlene O'Keke, who began to orientate me concerning things at the hospital and she also began to check my vital signs. She observed the severity of my condition and told me that she would do everything she could to help me. My physical condition was very severe. At this point, I was weaker than I had ever been since the onset of this disease. It seemed that every day, every moment and every second I deteriorated more.

I assured the nurse that "ALL IS WELL," even when it doesn't always appear to be well. We walk by faith, not by sight! My body is weak, but, thanks to God, my spirit is strong!

A humorous thing occurred as my wife and I talked with the nurse. The nurse began to issue supplies for me that night, including towels, sheets and a frilly hospital gown that was trimmed with pink, yellow and blue bows. I immediately concluded that probably she thought I was sicker than I really was and I was a very sick man. Upon questioning the nurse as to whether there was any attire available that would be more masculine, she advised me that this was it. I asked her if she could please check another floor to see if there were some tee shirts or pajamas that I could wear. She said that there wasn't anything else available. I very politely told her that, being a man, I wouldn't feel very comfortable in that gown and that I wasn't going to wear it and that she couldn't make me wear it because I knew what my rights were. I told her in a very nice way that I would have my wife to go to Wal-Mart and get me some tee shirts and pajamas to wear. The nurse smiled very broadly and told me that she understood. The word quickly spreaded to the nurses working other shifts that they could bring anything to Mr. Johnson's room but a frilly gown. I was teased by every nurse concerning that incident, but "All is Well!" My wife brought me some tee shirts and pajamas from my favorite store, Wal-Mart. Around 7:00 P.M. it suddenly dawned on me where I was. As my veins began to be pricked so that IV therapy could begin, and as darkness began to settle in, suddenly I realized that I was in a strange place and I would be away from my wonderful wife and children, and that I would not be going back home for awhile. A feeling of sadness and loneliness overwhelmed me, but I concluded that I must be strong and of good courage because "nothing in life is ever permanent, not even life itself, it's just temporary." God let me know that he would never leave me nor forsake me, and that "ALL IS WELL". He told me that He was not allowing this to happen to me to make me bitter but to make me better. I'm convinced of the fact that "circumstances do not make a man, they just reveal what he is made of."

Around 7:30 P.M. Nurse Margaret Washington entered my room and advised me that she would be my nurse until 7:00 A.M. the next morning. Because of the severity of my condition, she was basically in my room all night, monitoring my condition and calculating the amount of medicine that I was to receive in the IV. It became very tedious at times during the night because of the very specific dosages of various kinds of medication that I was started on. She consulted with other nurses, the doctor, and the pharmacist to be certain of the instructions. I very gratefully thanked her for the concern and compassion that she displayed toward me and my condition. I also thanked her for taking the time to consult with her colleagues before giving me the medication, rather than afterwards. She expressed great concern and let me know that I was in her prayers. She worked faithfully and diligently throughout the night making sure that I was as comfortable as possible. In an effort to make the best out of my illness and my situation, I pondered as to what I could do to help make things better for others, including those who cared for me, my family and for those who visited me. I also petitioned God, asking how I could take this stumbling block and turn it into a stepping stone. I began to talk to God, and in my deteriorated and gravely ill condition, I said, "God I know that I can't walk, I can't use my hands and legs, I know that I am in a very deteriorated condition, but not so much as to what I want you to do for me, but what can I do for you? God spoke to me and said, "I know the condition that you are in, I know that you are in a very physically deteriorated condition, but you still have breath in your body." This reminded me of **Psalms 150:6** which says:

"Let everything that hath breath praise the Lord. Praise ye the Lord."

God said, " At midnight tonight, your first night in the hospital, even though there are some who feel that you won't make it through the night, I want you to start a soul-saving revival right here in your hospital room." He let me know that there were many employees right there in the hospital that were lost and in despair. He let me know that many of them needed to be encouraged and inspired. He said that He wanted to use me to proclaim the gospel to them and to let them know that "No one is hopeless whose hope is in God." He told me to tell them to Keep Hope Alive! I said, "Yes Lord!" I saw this as an opportunity to practice what I had been preaching for 20 years. I had accepted the call to preach the gospel of Jesus Christ 20 years before my illness. So for 20 years I had visited sick rooms and death beds. I had talked to people who were suffering many things in their lives and I had always told them to put it in the hands of God, because God can do anything but fail. I had simply told them to "Keep Hope Alive." God let me know that He had allowed a great and wonderful opportunity to develop for me to take the medicine that I had given others for 20 years. I thanked Him in the midst of my condition for the great opportunity that He had afforded me to lift Him up. I began to reflect on how biblical characters dealt with their difficult situations and how God brought them through. I remember how Paul and Silas, while they were in prison, began to sing and pray unto God at midnight and the prison doors were opened and everyone's bands were loosed. I felt that if God did this for them at midnight, He could do something for me, for God has no respect of persons. In Acts, Chapter 16 and verses 25-26, it says:

(25) "And at midnight Paul and Silas prayed, and sang praises unto God: and the prisoners heard them". (26) "And suddenly there was a great earthquake, so that the foundations of the prison were shaken: and immediately all the doors were opened, and everyone's bands were loosed".

With this in mind I decided that I wouldn't go to sleep until after midnight because I wanted to be obedient and do the will of God. I felt that being obedient would be my ticket out of there. I was also reminded of what Jesus said in **St. John 9:4:**

"I must work the works of him that sent me while it is day: the night cometh, when no man can work."

So, at midnight I began to preach, to pray and to sing praises unto God. The nurses heard some noises in the room and felt they needed to check things out because some of them had concluded that I wouldn't live through the night. When they came in they realized that I wasn't thinking about dying, but rather, at midnight I began to praise God. They immediately joined in and began to praise God with me. This was the beginning of a 35-day

50

red-hot revival that was conducted from my hospital room, room 2344, at St. Vincent Medical Center, located in Little Rock, AR. I basically let them know that I was going to live until I die! And that it's not over until God says it's over.

The nurses and hospital staff began to look forward to coming in my room each night for midnight revival service. Some nights I would be asleep but they would come in and say, wake up preacher, it's midnight revival time. I would wake up and gladly start the revival. I had the greatest time of my life being in the hospital and at death's door. It gave me an opportunity to practice what I had been preaching for 20 years. I let them know that I was going to live!

God truly blessed, saved, delivered and healed. The revival continued both night and day as people came in and out of my room. God also told me to turn my hospital telephone into a prayer line. Calls came in from 6:00 A.M. in the morning until around 9:30 P.M. at night because that is when the phones were turned off for the night so that the patients could get some rest, although there would not be much rest for me because of my full evangelistic schedule. It gave me something positive to do while I waited patiently for the works of God to be made manifest. To God be the glory! The devil meant this illness for evil but God has turned it into good. I know that the devil could not have brought this affliction upon me without God's knowledge nor without God's permission. I simply concluded that God had given his permission for this muscle disease to come upon me and that "ALL IS WELL!" I have come to realize that for every minus in life, beside it there is always a plus, and the plus always outweighs the minus if we approach it from the right perspective. Even in adversity there is opportunity! Even though I was gravely ill, my first night in the hospital went exceptionally well with the help of God. Those who thought that I would not live through the night were amazed and astonished at the power of God. Every opportunity has a difficulty and every difficulty has an opportunity! God blessed me to look at the opportunities that He was allowing me to have in the midst of a difficult situation.

FIRST WEEK
(summary)

I entered the hospital around 4:45 P.M. on Friday evening, December 30, 1994. This was the day that a final diagnosis of dermatomyositis was made. This diagnosis was made after visiting several doctors during the day and also after having an electromyography (EMG) done at St. Vincent Medical Center. When I was admitted to the hospital I could not walk alone. I needed maximum assistance in getting in and out of bed. I had difficulty sitting up without my neck dropping down because of poor muscle control in my back and my neck. There was also very poor muscle control in my back and my legs. I needed maximum assistance from staff. I had much difficulty swallowing and in taking care of personal needs. During the first week of my stay in the hospital, I was totally confined to my bed with continuous IV therapy of high dosages of various types of medication to combat this rare disease of the muscles. I was a very, very sick man, but my faith in God would not allow me to look at how sick I was but rather how much power God had to heal me. So I proclaimed to myself and to all that I came in contact with that in spite of what was happening to me, "ALL IS WELL!"

My muscle enzyme level was over 30,000 points when I was admitted on December 30, 1994. The normal is around 250 points or below. This indicated that there was severe inflammation and deterioration of my muscles.

Shortly after being admitted to the hospital today, I received a telephone call from some good friends of mine. It was the Simpson family from Conway, Arkansas. Ms. Irene Simpson, a co-worker of mine, had heard that I was already in the hospital even before I was

52

admitted. She immediately called her daughter, Hazel Simpson, who is also a co-worker, and her sisters Shirley and Teresa and told them to do whatever they needed to do to find out where I was and how I was doing. This made me feel very good, knowing that so many people cared. About 5:15 P.M. the phone rang and it was Hazel and her sisters. They told me that they had called all the hospitals in the Little Rock area and that they finally found me. They were so happy that the mission that their mother had sent them on had been accomplished. About 5:45 P.M. Hazel, Shirley and Teresa entered room 2344 to see first-hand the condition that I was in. They were extremely saddened and highly concerned when they saw my deteriorated physical condition, but soon were relieved when they saw the extremely high and confident spiritual condition that I was in. I told them that in spite of how it looked and in spite of the physical condition that I was in, "ALL IS WELL!" I told them that I was going to "Keep Hope Alive!" They relayed the report to their mother and around 7:30 P.M. I received a call from her. She wanted to talk to me herself. Irene, Hazel, Shirley, Teresa and Teretha (who are twins) and the entire Simpson family kept in close contact with me throughout my hospital stay and until I had completely recovered from my illness. They still check on me periodically to make sure that "ALL IS WELL!" I am deeply grateful to them for their love and concern.

Nurse Margaret Washington observed on my first night in the hospital that the regular hospital bed that I was sleeping in was not conducive to a successful recovery. She recommended that because of my severe muscle condition the hospital should look at getting a more appropriate and a more comfortable bed for me. Ms. Washington was my nurse for the first two nights I was in the hospital, Friday night, December 30 and Saturday night, December 31. She returned to work the following Friday night, which was January 6 and found that no action had been taken toward getting me a more appropriate bed. She became very distraught and took it upon herself to consult with the staff again. The doctor was called and advised of the recommendation for a more appropriate bed. He gave his approval, and Saturday night,

January 7, around 10:00 P.M. I had a new bed that I refer to as the Cadillac of beds. I tell people that I came in sleeping in a Volkswagen but God put me in a Cadillac. This is a special air bed which makes you feel as if you are sleeping on a cloud, and the sound is like being inside the cabin of an airplane before it takes off. It is a state-of-the-art computerized bed with all sorts of features. It inflates, deflates and it slowly turns me if needed, every 30 to 60 seconds to help prevent bed sores and skin break-down. Ms. Washington came in and saw the bed, and was very happy and excited that her suggestion had been followed through on. This illness and affliction has been a great blessing to me. It has been heaven on earth. God is not allowing this disease to grip my body to make me bitter, but to make me better. I know that this too shall pass and "ALL IS WELL!" This illness has been made so much easier because of the love, the concern and the compassion that has been shown to me by the nurses, doctors and entire staff of St. Vincent Medical Center. In addition to the great medical team that God has given me, my wife Marie and my children Eric and Eboni have been exceptionally good to me, along with the rest of my family, co-workers, church members and friends from all walks of life. This kindness has also come from people who don't even know me but know someone who knows me. The support from everyone far and near has been over-whelming and outstanding. With this kind of support and the faith that I have in the God that I serve, I've got to pull through this. It's been very difficult but with the help of God I will make it!

God blessed me to start midnight revival services in my hospital room my first night. The revival has been going great this first week. God has really been blessing me as well as the hospital staff and all those who have come in and out of my room. God has also blessed me to turn my hospital telephone number into a prayer line for those who are sick or in distress. The devil meant this illness for evil but God has turned it into good! I realize that the only difference between a stumbling-block and stepping-stone is the way a person uses it. I am determined to turn this stumbling-block into a stepping-stone. I have found that you don't have to use it to

54

stumble over but you can use it to climb above your difficult situations in life. In any situation in life we can allow it to make us better or bitter. I have decided that I have a choice, and I have elected to become better because of what I'm going through, rather than to become bitter over it. I know that God has a great plan for my life. In order to receive or to help effectuate that plan, I must go through something. I have decided to count it all joy!

My mind is made up, and no matter what happens to me I am still going to trust God, and regardless of what lies ahead and in spite of what happens to me, I am assured and I am confident of the fact that "ALL IS WELL!"

During my first few days in the hospital my barber, Mr. James Works, came by to give me a much-needed haircut. I asked him to cut it short in order to make it easier to handle. My muscles are so weak in my arms and hands, to the point that I cannot comb my hair. God is blessing me anyway. Mr. Works has been my barber for the last 30 years, and I am very appreciative that he made a special trip to the hospital to cut my hair. Mr. Works first cut my hair in May 1964. That was another special trip that he made, it was to my house at #26 Burbank Drive, Little Rock, Arkansas. The reason for the special trip that time was because of a near fatal accident that I had on Wednesday, March 18, 1964. On that date around 8:00 A.M. on a Wednesday morning, I was run over and nearly killed by an automobile as I crossed Gilliam Park Road en route to the corner grocery store to get change for a dollar that my dad had given me. It was my duty that morning to get change and come back to the house to share it with my other brothers, so that they could have lunch money and bus fare to school. I made it back home about six weeks later, after having spent six weeks in Arkansas Children's Hospital. God spared my life and I was blessed to live to tell about it. The car ran over me, and in the process I suffered a severely mangled and broken left leg, with three large holes knocked in my left knee, one large hole in my right knee, injuries to my head, and multiple cuts, bruises and lacerations to other parts of my body. The impact of the accident left me in the middle of the road, severely mangled and bleeding profusely.

My leg was nearly detached from my body. I was 13 years old and was in the seventh grade at Booker Jr. High School in Little Rock, Arkansas. It was a miracle and a great blessing from God that I was not killed. The gentleman who ran over me never saw me and I never saw him. I had waited for a city bus to pick up passengers. Immediately after the bus took off going south, I attempted to cross the street and ran into the path of the car going north. Carolyn Morgan, who lived across the street from me, witnessed the accident and flagged the gentleman down to tell him that he had run over someone. In the excitement of the moment he put his car in reverse to hear what she was saying. As he backed up, he almost ran over me again as I lay critically injured in the middle of the road, but God stopped the car! I was shocked and confused about what had happened. Everything happened so quickly. As I evaluated my condition, I became hysterical and frightened to see that my left leg was barely attached to my body. I was also bleeding profusely from injuries sustained to both legs, my head, my arms, and my hands. I never loss consciousness. I never experienced very much pain because my body was numbed from the impact of the accident. Crowds of people gathered asking many questions and offering their assistance. The police, the ambulance and my family were notified of the accident. Family members were devastated by the news of the accident and ran swiftly to the scene to see for themselves what had happened. Tears and sadness overwhelmed them as they saw my bleeding and severely mangled body lying in the middle of the road. They were very grateful to God, as I was, that my life had been spared. Within moments I began to hear, from a distance, the screaming sounds of sirens from the police and the ambulance vehicles as they sped swiftly to the scene of the accident. My anxiety level increased tremendously because I didn't know what to expect nor what the outcome would be. The police arrived on the scene first and moments later the ambulance arrived and transported me to University Hospital where I was stabilized and then transported to Arkansas Children's Hospital later in the day. God was truly watching over me!

I was in Arkansas Children's Hospital from March 18, 1964 to April 30, 1964. I returned home in a body cast and was bedridden for most of the summer of 1964. My parents put me in a room next to a window so my friends could come to my window and talk to me. After the body cast was removed I was in a wheelchair and on crutches for awhile. A cousin of mine, Mr. Nathaniel Hendrix transported me from the hospital to my home in his station wagon and he also was so kind to take me back and forth to the hospital for my check-ups. The body cast prevented me from riding in a regular car.

By the help of God I eventually fully recovered from all injuries sustained from the accident. I lost no time out of school because, while in the hospital from March 18 to April 30, 1964, I had school in the hospital, and from April 30th to the end of the school year, I had school in my bedroom as I lay in bed, fully attired in a body cast. A teacher was sent to my house so that I would not miss any time from my school work. By September 1964 I was able to return to Booker Jr. High School as an eighth grade student. My legs were still very weak from the accident, but I thanked God that I was able to walk again. Many people felt I would never walk again after being so badly mangled as a result of the accident. God was just looking out for me. I've never had any trouble as a result of the accident. God has truly been good to me! PRAISE GOD!

During my first few days in St. Vincent's, my oldest brother Elder William Johnson came by to visit me. I had talked with him several times on the telephone before I entered the hospital, but he hadn't seen the condition that I was in. Each time he called the house I told him that "ALL IS WELL." I maintained the position that "all was well", even though my condition was deteriorating on a daily basis. I recognized the fact that we walk by faith not by sight. I also realized that all the faith I had in God when the sun was shining in my life must be put into action now that the storms were raging in my life. When William walked in he was shocked to see my physical condition, but very uplifted to see my spiritual condition. Even though I couldn't walk, use my hands well, or comb my hair, I still praised God!

Psalms 150:6 says:

"Let every thing that hath breath praise the Lord. Praise ye the Lord". This is what God is blessing me to do. I give all praise to God"!

Psalms 27:14 says:

"Wait on the Lord: be of good courage, and he shall strengthen thine heart: wait I say, on the Lord".

This is also what I am doing. I am patiently waiting on the Lord. I know that He is coming to my rescue. He promised never to leave me nor forsake me.

Psalms 40:1 says:

"I waited patiently for the Lord; and he inclined unto me and heard my cry".

Isaiah 40:31 says:

"But they that wait upon the Lord shall renew their strength; they shall mount up with wings as eagles; they shall run, and not be weary; and they shall walk, and not faint."

As my brother observed the critical physical condition I was in, he was in awe that regardless of that, I still said, "ALL IS WELL." I realize that without a test one cannot have a true testimony. God is giving me a testimony that I will be able to carry around the world.

What really struck him was that while he was in my room the nurse brought in my supper. The supper consisted of rice, chicken breast, other vegetables, bread, tea, coconut pie and an orange. Because I had very, very limited use of my hands, the nurse, Kelly May, cut up the chicken breast for me and made everything easily accessible to me. As she began to walk out of the room she asked me if I was going to eat my orange. I told her that I didn't think that I would. She then with much compassion said, "Well, I'll peel it for you." I knew that I didn't have the strength in my

58

hands to peel it, so I graciously thanked her and told her if she would peel it for me then I would certainly eat it. It was at this point that my brother really realized the severity of my condition. He teased me and said, here you are talking about all is well and you can't even peel an orange! I laughed and told him that in spite of all that, "ALL IS STILL WELL"! My brother William visited me several times while I was in the hospital. I also received visits from my niece Diane Jordan and her husband Earl and their son Samuel. Brother Clay Howell, brother Keith Hayes, and Elder Abram Bunting from my home church also visited me. This has certainly been in my favor. The nurses come in each day and each night and tell me that they had to really put up a fuss with the other nurses so that they could be the one to care for me.

This really made me feel good, knowing that there were so many people who didn't mind caring for me. Some of the nurses and staff who cared for me were: Margaret Washington, Joyce Larry, Nena Pittman, Tracey Vail, Larry Charles, Marcie Justice, Heather Ables, Kent Wilson, Serenda Jordan, Peg Lufkin, Tammy Warwick, Rhonda Pearson, Deidra Henderson, Roger Smith, Elizabeth Head, Cathy Peer, Peggy Wise, Debra Williams, Verdia Pittman, Bonnie Pauls, Willie Mae Burt, Steve Walker, Karla Outlaw, Pam McMahen, Gwen Kent, Patrice Clipp, Arnetta Barber, Darlene O'keke, Rosalyn Wallace, Lanetta Buckley, Cathy Quann, Donna Larch, Elaine Woods, Ann Odland, Patti Hedges, Kelly May, Tomeka Maddox, and many others. All of them were so kind and compassionate towards me, and all of them became part of my family and will forever hold a special place in my heart. As a small token of appreciation I always keep two big jars of my nurses' favorite cookies, crackers, fruits and candies on my night stand. Some of their favorite candies are Snickers, Milky Way, and Starbursts. They often come in my room throughout the day and night and feel very welcome to help themselves to the goodies, which is only a small token of my appreciation, gratitude and indebtedness to them.

My wife Marie and my brothers James and Clint Johnson and their wives Ozetta and Sharon replenish the jars when they start to get a little low. The nurses are very, very, appreciative of the goodies that are being provided for them.

I also had a great team of doctors that God blessed me with. They are: Dr. Raymond Miller, Internal Medicine; Dr. Christopher Adams, Rheumatologist; Dr. Joe Pevahouse, Kidney Specialist; Dr. Joe Hargrove, Cardiologist; Dr. Robert Abraham, Neurosurgeon; Dr. Coburn Howell, Neurologist; and Dr. David Rozas, Ophthalmologist. All of them are great physicians that God has entrusted my care to. I have been inspired and encouraged by all of them.

Many friends, family and co-workers have called or come by during my hospital stay including my lovely wife Marie, my wonderful children Eric and Eboni Johnson, my wonderful mother, Mrs. Laura Johnson, the number one dad in the world, my father Elder William Johnson, and his wife Ms. Rose. I also received visits and calls from the greatest family members in the world: my brothers William, Charles, Clint, James, Preston, Samuel and their families. My sisters Laverne, Queen Esther, Mary and their families also checked on me, as did Elder Jewel Withers Jr. and his wife Joyce, Elder Vernon Briscoe, Elder Willie Barnes, Elder Willie Houston, Elder W.E. McGowan and his wife Doris, Elder Jewel Thrower and his wife Debbie, Minister Stanley Ashley, and Elder James Tillman and wife. Many co-workers called or came by: my supervisor Ed Jennings and co-workers Shirley Crawford, Mary Jane Russell, Robin Steinmetz, Sharon Mohammed, Linda Henderson, Anetia Crenshaw, Carl and Janice Campbell, Tina J. Brown, Tina R. Brown, Cheryl Greenlaw, Gale Sasser, Diane Dillard, Lorraine Brown, Ms. Flora Perkins, Mother Alberta Bell, Mother Gaddie Dorbins and many, many others. God has truly and richly blessed me with so many caring people. Co-workers Alesia Holbrook, Joyce Rossi, Kaye Malcom, Stella Morris, Pamela Hancock, and Barbara Moore also checked on me this week.

The midnight revival services went on all this week. God is truly blessing both night and day. Even though I am in the hospital, I am having one of the greatest experiences of my life. I thank God for counting me worthy enough to suffer for him and "ALL IS WELL."

Second Week

(summary)

Week two took on a much better shape than week one. Noticeable improvements began to take place. Many, many prayers have gone up to God on my behalf and He has heard them and responded to them. My muscle enzyme level dropped significantly from over 30,000 points on December 30, 1994 to around 8,000 points this week. That is over 22,000 points it has dropped in little over a week. PRAISE GOD! During this week, my enzyme level did, however, go back up to around 10,000 points. Dr. Christopher Adams did become very concerned with this. He also discussed my situation with other physicians in the state and around the country as to what course of action to take next. He decided to put me on additional IV therapy for three days. It is a form of steroid medication that's very powerful and could have some very serious and dangerous side effects. With my consent and having been made aware of the possibility of what could happen if we tried this treatment, and what could happen if we didn't try it, both of us concluded that it would be in my best interest to proceed with it. After three days of treatment with this medication my enzyme level began to drop again. PRAISE THE LORD! I am being frequently monitored for any possible side effects such as damage to my liver, kidneys or heart. From reports that I've been receiving from my doctors, no side effects have been observed and "ALL IS WELL!" PRAISE GOD!

This second week of my hospital stay in room 2344, St. Vincent Medical Center, Little Rock, Arkansas has shown many significant improvements. I started receiving physical therapy twice a day. Therapy has been going great! Noticeable improvements in my mobility were made during this second week.

Physical therapy staff are assisting me in learning how to walk again and in how to use my hands and arms again. As a result of this disease I basically had lost the use of my hands, arms and legs and had to be retrained by the therapy staff. Again, the hospital staff has been exceptionally nice to me. My family, my co-workers from the Conway Human Development Center, my church members, and my friends from all over have been truly outstanding. God has blessed me with so many people who are encouraging me to hang in there! Tough times never last but tough people do! This has been heaven on earth! A quote that has inspired me is, "When life gives you lemons, make lemonade!" Another one is, "God does not allow us to go into deep waters to drown us, but so that we may learn to swim!" I am learning to swim through some very tempestuous and turbulent waters as a result of the disease that has attacked my body, and I am also learning how to make lots of lemonade, but "ALL IS WELL!"

On Thursday, January 12th, 1995, I was taken to surgery to have a muscle biopsy done on my left leg. Although it appeared that the correct diagnosis of dermatomyositis had been made, this was another conclusive method to rule out cancer as being a cause for my illness. It was concluded from the biopsy results that cancer was not a factor.

I was taken to the surgery holding area around 7:30 A.M. this morning. I did have some concerns about the surgery because it was my first experience with having surgery. I asked many, many questions of the doctors and nurses and they assured me all would be well. I do have a confession to make. The frilly gown that I refused to wear the day that I was admitted to the hospital was worn by me to surgery today. I pleaded my case against it for several days before the surgery, but I lost my case. The nurses assured me that immediately after surgery I would be able to change back into my tee shirt and pajamas.

Surgery began around 9:15 A.M. and was over around 10:15 A.M. As I was taken to surgery, I became very observant of the bright lights, the chilly temperature in the room and the masked surgeon and his assistant. More questions by me concerning my impending surgery appeared to have come out of nowhere as I observed my surroundings. Dr. Robert Abraham, the neurosurgeon who did the surgery, comforted and assured me that "all was well". I was awake during the surgery and heard the conversations by the staff and also heard the noises made by the instruments that were used for the surgery. My left leg was deadened and Dr. Abraham proceeded to make the approximately one inch incision on the area of my left thigh. Even though my leg was numb, I still felt the pressure from the incision being made and the pulling and tugging that was done to retrieve a piece of the muscle. Although I was not in any pain, I became very concerned over what I knew was happening and a distortion of my countenance or grimace began to show on my face. The doctor and nurses were good to me. They asked if I was experiencing any pain. I said, "No!" They said, "Why are you grimacing then?" I said, "It's just the thought." Just the thought of knowing what they were doing to my leg caused me to grimace. The surgery lasted about an hour but it seemed as if it lasted forever. Each time I thought it was over, they said we've got a little bit more to do. Electric shock waves penetrated up and down my leg, but I told myself, "ALL IS WELL." I breathed a great sigh of relief and I began to praise the Lord when Dr. Abraham finally told me that he had finished the surgery and that he was preparing to put the stitches in and that within a short period of time I would be taken back to my room. I thanked him and his staff for taking such good care of me and for answering my many questions and for making this experience as pleasant as possible. I returned to my room around 11:00 A.M. I immediately asked the nurses to assist me in getting out of that frilly gown and back into my favorite white tee shirt and dark blue pajamas. They got a big kick out of the fact that they got to see me in the gown that I refused to wear on admission day.

This week I received a great visit from Dr. Reginald Barnes, a cardiologist and good friend of mine for many years. He let me know that I was in his prayers and he encouraged me to keep the faith.

Another good friend of mine, James Yarbough, and his wife Linda came to visit me. I was really glad to see them. Both of them inspired me greatly. James, however, even though he did not show it, was very concerned and shaken by the condition that he saw me in. We have been good friends since childhood. I found out later that James had expressed to another good friend of mine, John Lovelace, that if he really wanted to see me alive again he really needed to get to the hospital as soon as he could. Of course John took James at his word and got to the hospital quickly. When John arrived to my room, he found me rejoicing and praising God, and he heard me say "ALL IS WELL!" I must admit that my physical condition did lead many people to believe that my departure was at hand, but I was convinced that this was only a test that God was allowing me to experience. I realize that "no test, no testimony; no cross, no crown". God is just giving me a testimony, one that I can carry around the world. John was very relieved when he saw me and, in spite of how I looked, he realized that "all was well".

We had a great visit. I am convinced that Paul was right in **Philippians** 1:21 when he said:

"For me to live is Christ and to die is to gain."

The Living New Testament version of **Philippians** 1:21 says:

"For to me, living means opportunities for Christ, and dying, well, that is better yet!"

Job says in **Job, chapter 13 and verse 15:**

"Though he slay me, yet will I trust him: but I will maintain mine own ways before him."

Job 19:25-27 says:

(25) "For I know that my redeemer liveth and that, he shall stand at the latter day upon the earth. (26) And though after my skin worms destroy this body, yet in my flesh shall I see God, (27) Whom I shall see for myself, and mine eyes shall behold, and not another, though my reins be consumed within me."

The midnight revival services continue and are in full swing this week. Many people are being blessed and as a result, my condition doesn't seem so bad. "ALL IS WELL!"

THIRD, FOURTH, AND FIFTH WEEK

The third week has been exceptionally great! My strength is returning. Physical therapy is going great. God is continuing to bless me. The revival as of this date is in the 21st day, I'm getting in and out of bed each day and I am able to do things that I couldn't do the day before. I have been conducting midnight revival services where staff gather around my bed for preaching, prayer, praise and worship service. I've been praying for the sick and for those who have come to visit me and have established a prayer line between 6:00 A.M. and 9:30 P.M. Staff and others are being blessed and God is getting the glory! I am able to walk without assistance during this third week of my hospital stay and "ALL IS WELL!" Dr. Christopher Adams has advised me that my enzyme level had dropped to below 5,000 points. Great news!

As of this date over 100 people have come to see me and over 100 more have called to check on me. This is a very conservative estimate. I received a wonderful visit from my father-in-law, Mr. Wilmer Page Sr., and from my brother-in-law, Mr. Wilmer Page Jr., both live in Rosston, Arkansas, about 100 miles from Little Rock. I was so happy that they took time out to come visit me. During this time I also received visits from my sister-in-law, Joyce Hawthorne, and her husband Rev. Jimmy Hawthorne and their children. Some of my friends, relatives and co-workers who called or came by were Shirlene Hasselback, Oliver and Laverne Haney, Bill and Cecilia Mitts, Rose Sullivan and Judy Weaver, Betty Hartsfield, Shirley Crawford, Betty Sue Baker, Margie Wofford, Margaret Hughes, Pat Lambert, Tom Johnson, Danny Gene Long and his wife Martha, Johnny and Martha Johnson, Margaret

Smiley, Tom Collie, Christy Loveless and her husband Billy, Raymond Lowe, William James Johnson, Barbara Moore, Ruth Griffin, Bert Presson, Elder Jerry Bradden and his wife Yvonne, Elder Lee Henry Williams, Bro. Harry Hayman, Elder Frederick Johnson and his wife Bernice, Minister Curtis Chunn and his wife Earnice, Elder Roy Blackmon, Elder George Gooden and son-in-law Brian Baker, Elder Paul Robinson, Rev. Lewis Campbell, Freida Marsh, Janice Smith and a call from my adopted sister Dee Swift who lives in Dallas, Texas. Many, many other people called or came by to see me during this time, including co-workers Stella Morris, Pamela Hancock, Anetia Crenshaw, Dorothy Maltbia, Felecia Bailey, Sharon Ames, Janet Thompson and friends, Elder Raymond Savage, Elder Doyle Moore and his wife Brenda, and Brother Arthur Drumgoole and his wife Gracie.

Even though I have been gravely ill, I must say that this has also been one of the greatest opportunities to minister to others that God has ever afforded me. I am deeply grateful to God for entrusting me with such a great responsibility and with such an enriching and rewarding opportunity! Week three has shown monumental improvements in my condition. Praise the Lord!

Thursday, January 19, 1995

Today, Thursday, January 19, 1995, has been an exceptionally great day for me. I am able to continually become more and more independent in my stay here in the hospital. I'm measuring my own input and output levels. The nurses used to have to do this. I took it upon myself to do this to help ease the duties of the nurses. I felt if I could do it myself, why bother someone else to do it. Physical therapy session went great today. I made significant improvements in mobility. My supervisor, Mr. Ed Jennings, and my secretary, Shirley Crawford, called me from work today, as they do practically everyday. I received a full regular paycheck today, which was great since I haven't been to work in almost a month. God has blessed me to be approved for catastrophic leave, which will allow me to continue to receive my paycheck until I return to work. It's been great being in the hospital. It's the next best thing to being in heaven. I glory in my affliction. Praise God!!! Paul said in **II Corinthians 12:9-10:**

(9) "And he said unto me, my grace is sufficient for thee, for my strength is made perfect in weakness. Most gladly therefore will I rather glory in my infirmities, that the power of Christ may rest upon me. (10) Therefore I take pleasure in infirmities, in reproaches, in necessities, in persecutions, in distresses for Christ's sake, for when I am weak, then am I strong."

I received several long-distance phone calls and visits today from friends, family, and co-workers. My brother Charles Johnson from Detroit made his usual two to three calls today to get a briefing on my condition. I received two to three calls from Verona, Italy today from my brother Samuel Johnson and his wife Nell. Calls have come in today from my sister Laverne Haney in Atlanta, Georgia. She also called several times last week to get a briefing on my condition. Get well wishes came in from my nieces Brenda Johnson and Brenda Mead.

Calls have come in this week from my sister Mary Johnson in Los Angeles, California, Dee Swift in Dallas, Texas, and from friends all over Arkansas. God has blessed me wonderfully this day. He stepped in my room at about 3:30 A.M. this morning and told me that I had been conducting services during the day and also some midnight revivals, and that I was running low on fuel, and that this personal revival this morning is for me. He stepped in from about 3:30A.M. to 4:30 A.M. this day, January 19, 1995 and poured out a great blessing on me. This is the twenty-first day of my continuous revival. This was the day that He filled me up again. He is getting me prepared for additional revival services. Praise God!

I have been touched by the Master and I am now ready to continue revival services during the day, and I am also ready to continue at midnight if it is the Master's will. Praise God!

My wonderful doctors, family, and friends have faithfully been with me through my illness. Dr. Raymond Miller, Dr. Chris

Adams, and Dr. Joe Pevahouse came by today and gave me some good reports. God is still blessing me daily!

Dr. Adams told me that I would get to go home one of these days. I thanked him but told him that "ALL IS WELL!" since I was in the midst of a red-hot 21 day revival and really wasn't ready for it to end yet. Praise God! So, the revival continues indefinitely!

I also made great strides today in my ability to function more independently. I have been able to get out of my highly technical computerized bed this week. When the staff press the right code to deflate the bed and when they let the rails down for me I am able to get out of bed without assistance. This is a very great and significant accomplishment because it used to take about three people to get me in the bed and three to get me out. This time it only took one person to push the button that I could not reach on the bed and God blessed me to do the rest.

Tonight God blessed me to achieve another very, very important and significant accomplishment. The staff had assisted me in getting out of bed and allowed me to sit up in a chair. I made the mistake of sitting up too long before asking the nurse to assist me in getting back in the bed. God had already blessed me to be able to get out of the bed earlier today with only minimal assistance from staff, but I had not yet learned how to get back into the bed on my own. I had been sitting up for a long time and was ready to go to bed around 10:30 P.M. By the way, this happened to be during the staff's shift change and briefing time. I pushed the nurses' button and asked that someone come to room 2344 to assist me in getting into bed. This may seem a little confusing but you have to remember that this is no ordinary bed. This is a highly specialized and computerized bed.

The nurses' button was pushed and I was advised that this was during shift change and that no one was immediately available to assist me, but that someone would be there just as soon as they possibly could. Since I didn't feel that it was necessarily an emergency that I get into bed at that particular time, I consented to wait until a staff member would be free to assist me. 11:00

P.M. had come and gone and no one had shown up to assist me. This is not a negative reflection on the staff because no one could have treated me as royally and as kindly as the staff of this hospital did. My only problem was that I waited until during shift change to want to get back in bed. Since no one had shown up by 11:15 P.M., and I was beginning to become very, very tired, God spoke to me and told me that this would be a great time for me to become creative. So, being the determined man that I am, and reflecting upon a quote that God put in my spirit while I was teaching a class at work, "DETERMINATION FINDS A WAY REGARDLESS OF WHAT'S IN THE WAY", I began to evaluate how I could master getting into bed without the assistance of staff, and also master pressing the right computerized button, which immediately inflates the mattress while the bed rises about two and a half to three feet from the level of the floor. So, still very slow and very weak in my legs and arms, I had to try to figure out how I could master pressing the button to elevate the bed and inflate the mattress and then make it to the side of the bed and jump on so I could ride up with the bed two and a half feet. By the way, I could have gotten in the bed while it was at a level near the floor where I could get into it, but without the mattress being inflated I would be lying on iron and metal because the mattress deflates completely. This would have been very uncomfortable and it would have been better for me to remain sitting up in my chair. I knew that being able to get in the bed alone would be a great challenge since I'm only five feet, five inches tall and suffering from severe muscle weakness in my arms and legs. I'm glad that I like challenges!

I studied how I would pull this off. I made practice runs to see how long it would take me to go to the foot of the bed and press the button and get back to the side of the bed to jump on it before it took off without me. I timed exactly the amount of time it would take to do this. I was very determined and confident that for the first time in twenty-one days, I could get into bed without the help of staff. The moment had come for me to see if I could pull this off. It was now 11:35 P.M. I deliberately did not press the nurses' button again because I realized that my time had come to become more independent in the hospital. I went to the foot of the bed and pressed the button. The mission was accomplished within seconds. I was able, by the help of God to press the button, rush to the side of the bed, and jump on it before it inflated and elevated. I rode up with it. Praise God!

This is just another miracle from God in this twenty-first day of my hospital stay. Also on this day, one of my coworkers, Sharon Mohammed, nicknamed me "Job Johnson."

It's now about 11:50 P.M. I need to get about a ten-minute nap, just in case I have to do a midnight revival!!!

Praise God! I got a ten to fifteen-minute nap and at approximately 12:10 A.M., members of the staff entered my room and the midnight revival started. God wonderfully blessed!

Friday, January 20, 1995

Today is Friday, day 22 of my stay in St. Vincent Medical Center in Little Rock, Arkansas. Today is also the 22nd day of a red-hot revival that started the same night that I entered the hospital.

My day started off great. PRAISE GOD! I got up around 4:30 A.M. and got cleaned up. My doctors, Dr. Raymond Miller and Dr. Chris Adams, always make early rounds to check on me. Another one of my doctors, Dr. Joe Pevahouse, normally makes rounds between 6:00-7:00 P.M. each night. Dr. Miller arrived first at about 5:20 A.M., and Dr. Adams arrived around 5:35 A.M. I thank God for the great doctors, nurses, and other staff that He has entrusted my care to. You could not ask for a better medical team than what God has blessed me with. These are great persons who believe and trust in God.

Things are going well. My muscle enzyme level is not really down like my doctors want it, but thank God it is not up like it was when I came in on December 30, 1994, when it was over 30,000 points. It went down to around 5,000 points on January 18 and then went back up to around 7,000 points today. I must confess that I am probably the cause of being in this dilemma as I reflect back over my busy schedule while I have been confined to

70

the hospital. A good friend and church member, Earl Williams Jr., came by during this time and helped to shave me. I was very grateful for his kindness. I also received calls or visits from Brother Dave Thomas and his wife, Sister Eddie Jean.

Yesterday was a very busy day for me. I went to physical therapy twice, visited and prayed with friends and family who came to visit, conducted revival services during the day, and prayed for people who called in on the prayer line. God impressed upon me to turn my hospital phone into a prayer line. The prayer line is open from 6:00 A.M. to 9:30 P.M. This is when the phones are on in the hospital room. I also worked on my daily journal until about 11:50 P.M. Then, as I stated in Day 21, I felt that I needed to take a nap for about 10 minutes because I felt a midnight revival coming on. At 12:10 A.M., the midnight revival started and God really blessed. Those who came in and out of my room were blessed, including me. God has been so good to me!

Today was a very tiring day for me as you can see. The preacher needs to modify his schedule and get some rest as my doctor suggested to me today, since I am in here for a very serious condition. He suggested that I get plenty bed rest so that my muscles can continue to heal. I promised him that I would be good and modify my schedule. So, I've been in bed most of today. I even got out of staying in physical therapy today. I went for the morning therapy session and stayed for only 20 minutes. I told the therapists that I was very, very tired, and the doctor advised me to get plenty of rest. I finally had to confess to them about the midnight revival. I did get excused from my afternoon therapy session so I could get some bed rest. During the morning therapy session my therapist, Mary Beth McDonald, praised me for doing a good job on my hand exercises. I then praised her for praising me and then I asked her if she had any M&Ms to give me for a positive reinforcer. She came out with a big bowl of different colored M&M's. They were great! I thanked her and then I finished my hand therapy session and was wheeled back to my room by physical therapy employee Willie Johnson. I stayed in bed for the rest of the day. At about 3:00 P.M., therapist Karen

James came by my room to discuss future therapy sessions scheduled to begin on Monday, January 23rd. I told her that my battery had run down but with plenty of rest over the weekend my battery should be recharged by Monday.

My wife Marie and my children Eric and Eboni came to visit me tonight. It was a great visit. Eboni is spending the night with me in the hospital tonight. She is so happy, and of course Dad is too. Also during this time, I received calls or visits from co-workers and friends: Janice Smith, Jesse Mae Lofton, Evada Thomas, Joe and Linda Robinson and their son Edwin, Mary and Rosalyn Bogard, and many others.

The nurses and doctors have encouraged me to modify my revival schedule, which I've done. So, I guess I will have to pass up the midnight revival that I had planned for tonight. But, "ALL IS WELL!"

Another important incident of the day was that one of my nurses told me that one of her patients had a stroke in his room this morning and passed away and the family is very distraught. The nurses suggested that the family come and talk with the man of God in room 2344. The family came down and God blessed me to counsel and pray with them. God really poured out and blessed them. They left rejoicing and praising God.

It is now 11:10 P.M. Eboni has gotten sleepy, and I am getting sleepy. So, since there is no midnight revival planned for tonight, I guess this is it for Day 22 of the red-hot revival in room 2344. God has truly blessed me during my hospital stay. He has also blessed all those who have been a blessing to the man of God in room 2344.

God Bless and Good night!!!

Saturday, January 21, 1995

Good morning! This is Saturday, day 23 of the red-hot revival in room 2344 3 NW, St. Vincent Infirmary Medical Center, Little Rock, Arkansas. About 3:00 A.M. this morning I had a severe episode of coughing. Eboni was awakened by it and became very alarmed and concerned. I assured her that "all was well". The coughing soon stopped and both of us were able to go back to sleep.

Well, day 23 is going great, except that there was no midnight revival last night. The preacher promised that he would curtail his activities but the revival in some way goes on both day and night. The nurses stated that they could tell that the midnight revival did not take place because they were confronted with so many problems that they felt would not have occurred had the revival taken place. They said the revival must continue tonight, for sure!

Today has been a great day for me. My wife and daughter were here to see me today. My brother-in-law Louis Page and his wife Wanda and their children, Pam and Corey, came to see me today. They drove over 100 miles to visit with me. We had a great time!

Several of my friends from *Acts 2:4 Church of God In Christ* here in Little Rock came to see me tonight, along with my pastor, Elder Jewel Withers, Jr., pastor of *Williams Temple Church of God In Christ,* Little Rock. Friends from *Rosedale Church of God In Christ* here in Little Rock also came to see me tonight as well as friends from *Victory Temple Church of God In Christ,* Little Rock. Friends from my job, the Conway Human Development Center, also came.

My brother, Clint Johnson, and his wife Sharon came tonight, along with Sharon's mother, Mrs. Gracie Carter. We talked and prayed and had a wonderful time in the Lord. I have received get-well wishes from my sister-in-law in Prescott, Arkansas, Joyce Banks and her husband Michael, and my brother-in-law Willie Page and his wife Dorothy.

A very touching incident happened tonight. While all my friends were still in the room, one of my nurses, who works the 7:00 P.M. to 7:00 A.M. shift, came in about 6:15 P.M. She had a very difficult day today. She came to room 2344 to look for the man of God. She was advised that I had a room full of company. She pressed her way in and she said "I'm sorry, I'll have to apologize to your visitors but I need you to pray for me." We all joined in prayer for her. She left rejoicing and praising God. God is so great! To God be the glory!

Well, it is now 11:02 P.M. I'm in bed compiling my journal for day 23, which has been a great day for me! I've been blessed and touched by all those who have visited with me today and tonight. "ALL IS WELL"!

I must rest now in order to be ready for the midnight revival that I feel coming on.

Great news today my muscle enzyme level is down from over 30,000 points when I came in on December 30, 1994, to 4,000 points today, January 21, 1995. The normal range is around 250 points or below. I still have a long way to go, but with the help of God I will get there!

Sunday, January 22, 1995

Today marks the 24th straight day of my stay in room 2344, St. Vincent Infirmary Medical Center, Little Rock, Arkansas. God has really been blessing mightily. He has proven Himself over and over again and He has shown me that He is the faithful God that we say He is. Again, this hospital stay with this affliction has been one of the greatest things that have happened to me in my 44 years and 4 months of living. Just a little note that I would like to share with you. According to the doctors and man's projection, there should not even have been a Roy Johnson born. My mother told me that there were severe complications with her pregnancies before me and with her pregnancy with me, and that I was given very little chance of being born. I'm so glad that in matters of this sort man can only give his feeble opinion, but God gives the facts. God said there would be a Roy Johnson born, and I am he. My mother, being very distraught over the news that she might lose me, went to a man of God whom she had much faith and confidence in and asked him to pray for her. He prayed for her and told her that not only would I be born but that I would be a blessed child. From talking with my mother I have concluded that she probably had too much faith and confidence in the man of God. He prayed for her and told her that all would be well for her and her little one in spite of what man projected. The only problem was that about two months before I was to be born, the

74

man of God in whom she had so much faith died. This devastated my mother because she was depending on him more so than she was depending on God. This is something that all of us need to be very careful about. It is okay to have a certain amount of trust in man, but our ultimate trust should be in God. Man is limited but God is unlimited!

After the man of God passed away it kind of shook her faith to a degree. Being deeply hurt and saddened over the death of the man of God, she began to question God as to what she would do now, that the man of God was dead. God responded and said, "MY CHILD, I AM HERE." This gave my mother great consolation, and her faith was restored and increased. Two months later, a healthy, screaming little baby boy by the name of Roy Henry Johnson was born on August 30, 1950. I was born in the bedroom of our house at 717 E. Harrison Street, Stuttgart, Arkansas. Upon the miraculous birth, happiness filled the house because many, many prayers had been answered and God had blessed bountifully. He brought my mother through a very turbulent pregnancy. I praise God for giving me the wonderful opportunity to be born to such great parents as William Johnson, Jr. and Laura Elizabeth Crews Johnson who are now 86 years old and 82 years old. I also thank God for giving me a chance to be born into the greatest family on earth, with all of my wonderful brothers and sisters.

As I said earlier, today has been a great day for me, I reflect back on how great God has been to me, even before I was born.

A midnight revival took place around 12:05 A.M. this morning when two nurses came into my room for preaching, prayer, praise and revival service. God blessed all of us in a great way and they left rejoicing and praising God.

Today at approximately 10:00 A.M., Nurse Steve Walker entered my room and told me that it was snowing outside. I got up from my bed and walked over to my third floor window and admired the beautiful, large snowflakes that passed by my window sill. It brought back memories of my childhood days when I would often go to the window and peer out at the weather conditions but could not go out. The child in me was very excited and anxious about wanting to go out and play in the beautiful snow. Although my condition prevented me from doing that, the great nursing staff of St. Vincent went out and threw a few snowballs and brought some snowballs back to my room so that I could experience in some similitude what was happening on the outside. I praise God for them! Two of the nurses were Nena Pittman and Tracey Vail. They were my nurses on a regular basis while I was in the hospital. Because of the six-inch snowfall today, I requested that my wife and children not come to the hospital to visit me. I asked her to go to the store and stock up on groceries in case they couldn't get out for a few days. She went to the store and stocked up for a week or so. That rested my mind that all was well with them. She also got a full tank of gasoline.

I really didn't expect any family to visit today because of the snowfall and I certainly did not expect anyone else to visit. My brother James made a valiant attempt to come by. He called around 10:00 A.M. and told me that he was on his way, but because of the very treacherous road conditions, he turned back at the first exit he came to. He called to express his regret for not being able to come. My brother Clint called. He decided to call to check on me from the comfort of his home to see if I had a dire emergency. Upon being advised that all was well, I noticed that he breathed a sigh of relief that he wouldn't have to come out into the cold, snowy, and icy weather. He was a little more relaxed in his conversation after he found out that "all was well".

As I lay in my bed content that there would probably be no visitors today, I heard a knock at my door and in came two friends and church members Larry and Dian Hicks. They had been to church and came through the snow to visit me. It really lifted my spirit greatly! I had resigned myself to just receiving phone calls today, but God blessed! On one of Dian's earlier visits to the hospital, she noticed that my hair had not been combed. When I told her that I was not physically able to comb it, she readily combed it for me. She didn't know that my condition had deteriorated to that point. I graciously thanked her because, not only did I look better, I felt better by having my hair combed.

The doctor still has me on strict bed rest and chair rest so that my muscles can heal. Although I have rested my leg muscles I'm still conducting day and night revival services. Many have been blessed, souls have been saved, bodies have been healed, blinded eyes have come open, deaf ears have been unstopped and the dead have been raised. Many people are walking around spiritually dead. Many have eyes but can't see, ears but can't hear, and many have legs but are lame in the spirit. God is richly blessing! I'm glad He counted me worthy enough to allow this trouble and this affliction to come upon me.

News that my muscle enzyme level is at 4000 points today is good news considering the fact that it has dropped over 26,000 points over a three-week period. It had dropped earlier to around 5000 points, then it went back up to around 9000 points. Praise God that it is down to 4000 today. Being exiled to my room has helped a lot, and the bed rest is helping my muscles to heal. Praise God!

I had been up on my legs too much, walking back and forth to visit my nurses at the nurses desk, walking my visitors up the hall to see them off, and from shaking hands and telling people that "ALL IS WELL," as well as from going from room to room praying for the sick and telling people to "KEEP HOPE ALIVE." I had forgotten, that, I too was suppose to be sick. I am reminded of a quote by Ralph Waldo Emerson that says, "No one can sincerely try to help another without helping himself" I have been truly blessed by my efforts to help others.

For the last two days I've been getting into a deluxe computerized bed by myself. God blessed me to make another major accomplishment today. A couple of days ago He blessed me to figure out a way to get into the bed alone, and today Sunday, January 22, 1995 He blessed me to figure out a way to get out of this bed alone. You have to remember that my muscles are still very weak and frail, and that I'm still barely able to stand up and get around. I'm still in a very weakened condition in both upper and lower extremities, but I determined that if God could allow me to be creative enough to get into the bed, He could give me that same determination to be creative enough to get out of bed.

Praise God! I successfully got out of bed alone today. God just keeps on doing great things for me!

The nurses on the night shift have been concerned about me tonight because they haven't heard from me. I used to have to push the nurses' button to call for them to do everything for me. Two or three nurses would have to come to help get me out of bed and to help get me back into bed. I think you can understand now why I am so excited about all of this because today by the help of God I can do all of this alone! God has been so good to me and He is blessing me in spite of what the devil has tried to do to me. How great Thou art!

I received many phone calls today from many people including my wife and children, my mother Mrs. Laura Johnson, my dad Elder William Johnson and his wife Ms. Rose, my brothers James, Clint and Charles and friends from work and others who have called to check on me. I also talked to my Aunt Bessie Blake from Prescott, Arkansas today. She has been very concerned about me and has been calling the house. I called her tonight and relieved her mind that "all is well" with me. I wanted to know if it was well with her. She advised me that she had fallen and had gone to the doctor a few days ago. She stated that the doctor looked at her and told her "You really had a good fall," and charged her account for his services. By the way, she also told me that he said that nothing was broken. She is in her 80s and "all is well"!

At 4:03 A.M. today, I made a special birthday card for one of my wonderful nurses, Ms. Peg Lufkin, who God blessed to help keep me from dying on my second night in the hospital. The side effects of some of the medication that I was on caused my lungs to fill with fluid, and I was not able to breathe very well. It seemed that every breath would be my last one. Ms. Lufkin stayed with me until the crisis was over. She was so proud of her home-made, spur-of-the-moment birthday card. During the crisis, Ms. Lufkin asked me if I wanted a Shasta drink. I very pitifully said "No Ma'am. I want a Sprite." She gladly accommodated me.

It is now 9:20 P.M. I must get to bed and get some sleep because I feel a midnight revival coming on! God bless and good night.

Monday January 23, 1995

Well, I did get some rest last night until approximately 11:55 P.M. when a nurse entered my room to check my vital signs and we began to talk about the goodness of God. The revival started at 12 midnight. I began to have a flashback to December 29, 1974, when God called me to preach the gospel. It spread from there into a preaching, praying, praising and rejoicing service. I also reflected on my favorite song, "I Won't Complain." I didn't sing it, but I was able to recite publicly the words to it. God poured out His spirit and all were blessed tremendously. God is good and good is God! Take one "o" out of good and you've got God, add it back and you've got good! **Praise God!** He is Good! And He is God!

It is now 2:40 A.M. The revival was so great that my sleep escaped me. I decided that I would begin today's journal early. This is Monday, day 25 of the red-hot revival that is taking place in room 2344, St. Vincent Medical Center, Little Rock, Arkansas. I must get some rest so that I can be briefed by my doctors at 5:30 A.M. about my condition and the progress that I am making. Good night or good morning once again. God has been so good to me and so faithful to me. I have concluded that for some reason or another, God is rewarding me in the midst of my troubles for some reason unknown to me; but I am certainly enjoying the trip. This has been heaven on earth to me. I'm reminded of what the bible says in **Romans 8:18:**

> *"For I reckon that the sufferings of this present time are not worthy to be compared with the glory which shall be revealed in us."*

Also, **I Peter 4:12-13** says:

> *(12) "Beloved think it not strange concerning the fiery trial which is to try you, as though some strange thing happened unto you":*

> *(13) "But rejoice, inasmuch as ye are partakers of Christ's sufferings; that, when his glory shall be revealed, ye may be glad also with exceeding joy".*

79

2 Timothy 2:3 says:

"Thou therefore endure hardness, as a good soldier of Jesus Christ."

As of this date and time January 23, 1995, at 2:55 A.M., over 300 people have come to visit me and over 300 people have called me. These are very conservative figures. Many more have attempted to call but have had difficulty getting through. For some it has taken two or three days for the phone to be free for them to speak with me. Thank God for so many caring people!

I've received over 250 get well cards and letters and other gestures of love. I have been deeply touched by the outpouring of love from everyone and I am so glad that I had a chance to live to see it. People are giving me my flowers while I live. I'm reminded of a poem *Flowers for the Living* that says:

Flowers for the Living

I would rather have a little rose from the garden of a friend than to have the choicest flowers, when my stay on earth must end.

I would rather have one pleasant word in kindness said to me than flattery when my heart is still and life has ceased to be.

I would rather have one loving smile from friends that I know are true than to have tears shed around my casket when I bid this world adieu.

So bring me all your flowers today, whether white or pink or red. I would rather have one blossom now than a truckload when I'm dead.   Author Unknown

I heard this poem recited by a good friend of mine and deacon of our church, Deacon Davis Young.

I tell people that the old Roy Johnson has moved he doesn't live here anymore. With the great outpouring of love, concern and compassion, the new and improved version of Roy Johnson is here now.

Praise God! It's 3:02 A.M. I must get some more sleep but I've got to tell you this. It's now 3:10 A.M. in the morning, God has just worked another daily miracle for me. As I got out of my bed, with no assistance and without having to call the nurses for help, I decided that I would exercise my faith by getting into the shower alone for the first time in my 25 day stay here. The muscles in my legs had been so weak before this morning that I could not raise them above the threshold to get into the shower. I always needed some assistance. Even though it is 3:14 A.M. and not time to shower, I decided I would exercise my faith and see if I could raise my legs to get into the shower. Praise God, I was able to do it! This is great accomplishment from not being able to walk when I came in on December 30, 1994. This was just a rehearsal for 7:00 A.M. this morning when I plan to take a shower alone and without any assistance from anyone. The physical therapy staff has been teaching me how to walk again and how to use my hands again. They have also been teaching me how to get into and out of bed, how to get into and out of a chair, and many other things that I had lost the ability to do due to the disease that severely affected many of my muscles. I am also able to hold my head up once again. At one point the muscles in my neck were so weak that I was not able to hold my head up for long periods of time. God is blessing so wonderfully!

Again, I must try to get some sleep unless another miracle takes place before I get a chance to. My doctors should be in around 5:30 A.M., to brief me on my condition.

It is now 3:17 A.M., but I must relate another miracle that God worked yesterday. A nurse who was off for two days called me and said, "I guess I am going to have to start believing in miracles because I see one unfolding right before my eyes." She saw me when I came in praising God and couldn't walk and couldn't raise my hands and was in a very weakened and critical condition and she has watched me as God is raising me up to walk and to function again, and I'm still praising God!

It is now 3:38 A.M. and I'm still desperately trying to get back to sleep but the midnight revival did something very special for me and I am still excited about it, and the miracles and blessings just keep on coming!

My next communication with you should be around 7:00 A.M. after I take my first shower alone in 25 days, unless another miracle takes place before then.

It's been a great but very busy day today! I finally got my shower alone at 5:00 P.M. today and then I put on my number one cologne, which is Stetson. It's been stated that the aroma of the Stetson floats down the hallway from room 2344 to the nurse's desk and they have been overwhelmingly impressed with it. I shall continue to wear the Stetson!

Around 7:15 P.M. I received a visit from my co-worker Clara Tucker and her daughter Christie. A special church service was started after we conversed about the goodness of God and how God was giving me a miraculous recovery. We talked about the troubles that I had experienced, but I told them, "I won't complain." I told God that I had lost the use of my hands and legs, but I said to Him, "Lord whatever You do, don't take Your spirit away from me." Through it all God has allowed His spirit to be alive and well within me. I truly thank Him for that because, with God's spirit dwelling within me, I can scale the highest mountain and I can swim the deepest sea and I can go through, around, over or under any trouble that may confront me. Paul says in **Philippians 4:13:**

"I can do all things through Christ which strenghteneth me."

While we continued to converse, Christie told me that she knew the words to the song "I Won't Complain." I immediately asked her if she would sing it. The spirit of God began to fill the room and we began to praise and magnify God!

As we were in the midst of the service, one of my doctors, Dr. Joe Pevahouse, entered the room and began to praise God with us. We had a wonderful time and everyone received a special blessing from God. Christie's melodious voice rang down the hallway and attracted the attention of another patient across the hall from me. He said that he was so touched by what he had heard in room 2344 that he wanted to come over and enjoy the Lord with us. The very interesting and intriguing thing about his visit was that, he said, while he was sitting in his room and heard the singing, he recognized the voice of the person doing the singing, and as he entered the room he recognized Christie. He had seen and had heard Christie singing the same song a week earlier at a high school beauty pageant that Christie was a contestant in. The song was done as a part of her talent. How interesting! Not only was that part interesting but as he and I began to share testimonies he expressed to me that I probably had never met a man like him before. This was also very interesting! As the testimony unfolded he expressed to me that he was a man who had two hearts beating in his chest. He was right; I had never met a man or woman with two hearts. He expressed that he had the heart of a young teenage male, piggy backed to the heart of a middle-age woman beating in his chest, and these two hearts were responsible for helping to keep him alive. He had received a couple of heart transplants a few years earlier. He was in the hospital for some minor complications he had experienced but he seemed to be doing well and he was discharged the next day, and "ALL IS WELL"! I went to his room the next day before he was discharged and we prayed together and bade each other God-speed as we parted.

Day 23 continued to be an exciting and enriching day for me. Around 8:00 P.M. tonight I received a visit from my supervisor, Mr. Ed Jennings and his wife Susan, and his twin sister Edna Wilson. We had a great visit. I also received a visit tonight from my co-workers Danny Gene Long and his wife Martha. My pastor, Elder Jewel Withers Jr., also came by as he has so graciously done practically every day since I have been here. My wife Marie and my daughter Eboni also came by tonight.

I guess I had better get a little rest before midnight, because I feel a midnight revival coming on!

I have had a very wonderful day!

Tuesday, January 24, 1995

There was no midnight revival tonight as of yet, but nonetheless God woke me up at midnight anyway. No one came for service, so I sang and prayed. While I was up on my feet, Nurse Gwen Kent peeped in to see what was happening at midnight.

Uh oh, 12:18 A.M.; more nurses showed up, but all was well with them from God having blessed in previous midnight revival services. We chatted for a moment and they left. I read my Bible and read a few excerpts from the book *Chicken Soup for the Soul.* "ALL IS WELL!"

My muscle enzyme level has been going up and down. This has been a great concern for the doctors. I think I have discovered one of the reasons for this that I am going to have to correct. Since I have gotten strong enough to walk some, I have been going up and down the hospital praying for the sick so they could go home to their families so someone else could have their bed. I wanted to keep mine for a few more days though, because God was doing so many great things at the hospital. I think reducing my evangelistic activities and resting my legs would help.

1:15 A.M. Day 26. I just finished reading my Bible and some excerpts from *Chicken Soup for the Soul. I* was richly inspired after reading **Psalms 46** and some motivational passages from *Chicken Soup for the Soul.* God is still blessing!

I got out of bed for a moment, and upon returning I was inspired by God to improve the way that I get back in bed. I used to, prior to day 26 at 1:15 A.M., walk to the back of the bed, push the button and then run and jump in it before it goes up. I just discovered that I could sit on the bed, reach to the back of the bed, push the button, lean back, scoot up and ride up and be in a perfect position for a good night's rest. God has done it again! I'm expecting him to do other things for me on day 26.

The showers are to continue on a daily basis now. No more only having two in twenty-five days. Praise God from whom all blessing flow. Just a word of encouragement to all. I have never gone untidy in all of those twenty-five days. I just was not physically able to get in the shower. Just a word to let you know that "ALL IS WELL!" Good night; it's 1:24 A.M.

It is now 3:45 A.M. I had to get up for a moment and God revealed to me that if I were able to sit on the bed, reach down to the computer panel, and push the button to elevate it while I was already in the bed, so that I wouldn't have to do that running and jumping in the bed like I started off doing, why not follow the same procedure on getting out of bed, so I won't have to jump two feet like I have been doing. He said, "Do the same thing to get out of bed that you did to get in." This really doesn't make sense unless you were there! Thanks be to God! Now it's no problem at all getting out of bed. Praise God! It's now 4:25 A.M. I must get some more rest. My doctors will be in to brief me on my condition between 5:15 A.M. and 5:45 A.M. After being in the hospital for 26 days I have had a lot of time to become very imaginative and very creative. Stay tuned for more miracles!

Day 26 went great!

As I have shared with you before, being sick has been one of the greatest things that ever could have happened to me. It's given me an opportunity to reflect back on a lot of things in my life: the great and wonderful people I've met, the wonderful wife of 21 years that I married, and my two wonderful children, who have been a great blessing to my life. Eboni is thirteen and Eric is seventeen. He is a senior at J.A. Fair High School in Little Rock. Eboni is an eighth grade student at Mablevale Junior High in Little Rock. Eric, for the first time in his life, has made the honor roll both nine weeks this year. I'm exceptionally proud of his accomplishments. Keep up the good work, Eric and Eboni!

Day 26 has been relatively quiet. I got to leave out of the hospital briefly today. This is the first time I have been outside to smell the fresh air and enjoy the beautiful sunshine in 26 days. As a result of the muscle disease and medication, white spots appeared in one of my eyes. My doctor sent me across campus to Blanford Eye Center to get an Ophthalmologist to check it out. "ALL IS WELL"! I was seen by Dr. David Rozas. He was a very kind gentleman.

I would like to encourage you not to take anything in life for granted, whether it is your life, health, family, job, friends or whatever the case may be. Appreciate and show appreciation now for what you have. Don't grumble and complain about what you don't have, just be thankful and grateful for what you have. Don't ever envy or covet what others have. Be thankful and happy for them!

I've always told my classes at work and I mention to people everywhere that at any time in our life we could become in a situation where we are down, disabled, or in a situation in life where we cannot function as we previously have.

Sunday, November 20, 1994, I began to find myself experiencing severe muscle weakness and spasms in my right leg. I was at church rejoicing and praising God during the morning worship service. After leaving the pulpit to go out and pray for people in the audience, I noticed some severe weakness in my right leg. As I attempted to enter the pulpit again, I noticed that my right leg was so weak that it was difficult for me to raise it up to the level of the step. In an effort not to make it obvious to the congregation, I was able to force my leg upon the step and make it back into the pulpit. At that point I began to seek additional medical attention because my condition was steadily deteriorating. Now I am hospitalized, suffering from a life-threatening muscle disease. We never ever know what will happen to us in life, so be thankful for every moment that God gives you. "Your life is God's gift to you; what you do with it is your gift to God!"

An employee from the physical therapy department came by and did therapy with me in my room this morning and this evening. They have done a great job!

As I sat in my chair around 7:18 P.M. on day 26, a great friend and co-worker, Tina J. Brown, and her daughters Leah and Jaclyn came by to visit me. It was her birthday, but she still found time to stop by for a visit. Also, another good friend and co-worker, Chaplain George Andrews, came to visit me today.

It is now 10:30 P.M. Good night and God bless!

Wednesday, January 25, 1995

There was no midnight revival last night. The preacher retired at approximately 10:30 P.M. and slept through time for the revival. I guess the preacher needed some rest.

Day 27 started around 5:25 A.M. when Dr. Chris Adams came in to brief me on my condition. He stated that I'm progressing well. The problem seems to be that my muscle enzyme level is remaining around the 4,500 level but having been over 30,000 points on December 30, 1994, I'm grateful for the wonderful progress. The higher my enzyme level is, the weaker I am. The lower it goes the stronger I get. So I think you get the point about the significance of the going down of my enzyme level, but "ALL IS WELL"! I expressed this to Dr. Adams. I advised him that God is not finished with me yet. I'm in the midst of twenty-seven day red-hot revival and neither God nor I am ready to close it out. PRAISE GOD!!! I need a few more days!

At approximately 6:10 A.M. this date, a nurse entered my room and we discussed how God had worked a miracle in her life after having brain surgery in a very delicate area of her brain about eight years ago. God miraculously gave her a great recovery and she is working every day and doing great. This helped to increase my faith concerning the disease that has attacked my body. I know that "ALL IS WELL!"

She also related a very beautiful story to me after I shared a quote with her about hatred. The quote is that:

"Hatred can be acid that does more damage to the vessel in which it is stored than to the object on which it is poured."

This brought a thought to her mind about an incident that she experienced with her little child when he saw a black person for the first time. His response was, "Mommy, there is a black person. Why did God make black people?" said the little five-year-old child. The mother responded, "If you were God and you looked out from heaven above and only saw white flowers, wouldn't you want it more colorful and more beautiful?" "Yes," replied the little lad.

"Well, this is what God has done. He wanted to make the world more colorful, so He made all kinds of people." The little lad was satisfied with the answer and was rested in his spirit after getting such a wonderful and colorful illustration of why we may have some things different but so many, many other things in common. For one thing, we all have the same Father which is in heaven.

When the opportunity presented itself for the young lad to prove that he understood his mother's wonderful explanation, he took full advantage of the situation. Once after the beautiful illustration, the little lad and his mother were riding a bus and a black lady boarded the bus and sat down close to them. Looking very intently at the black lady and knowing what his mother had shared with him, he very eagerly wanted to prove to his mother that he had understood what she had expressed to him. He looked at the lady and said, "I know why you are black." She was shocked and inquired as to why. His response was that God didn't just want a garden full of white flowers but He wanted to add some color to it. The lady smiled very broadly at the little lad and very graciously thanked him for the wonderful explanation that he had given her. He was so proud of himself for remembering what his mother had taught him, and she was so proud of him for remembering what she had said, exactly the way she had said it. Everyone, including the black lady, parted with big smiles on their faces.

God has richly blessed during this day. Breakfast trays arrived around 8:30 A.M. I sat in my chair and ate breakfast. After finishing breakfast I remained in my chair and dozed off to sleep. Upon waking up there was a beautiful lady standing in front of me and had watched me as I slept. As I looked in the big beautiful brown eyes of this lovely lady, and as I became focused on her, I realized that it was my lovely wife of 21 years. PRAISE GOD!

She gave me a surprise visit and even went with me to physical therapy at 9:30 A.M. She left around 12 noon to go to work. It was a great visit! She and my daughter Eboni returned at approximately 6:30 P.M. for another great and wonderful visit. During this time I also received calls or visits from friends and co-workers, Barbara Lorance, Anita Hauser, Eileen Hauser, Harry Hayman, Elaine Woods, Kim Dickey, Joy Crawford, and many others.

Another very exciting situation happened on day 27 of the soul-saving revival in the hospital. One of the nurses entered my room, and wanted to know what she must do in order to be saved.

I explained the plan of salvation to her and gave her an opportunity to give her life to Jesus. She had been caring for me and observing me for the past 27 days. She called me up about two weeks ago and told me that she guessed that she was going to have to start believing in miracles because she sees that God is working one right before her eyes. We continued to discuss the scriptures and God's great love for her. We will continue our prayers for her that God will continue to open up her understanding.

Thursday, January 26, 1995

There was no midnight revival last night. The preacher's busy schedule during the day has left him exhausted at night. I've been exiled to my room by the doctors and nurses since Friday, January 20, 1995. I probably had been a little too active in going up and down the halls praying for the sick and the afflicted and not giving my muscles a chance to rest. I was trying to help get some of these sick people well so they could go home to their families.

The doctor put me on complete bed rest. He told me when I'm not in the bed that I'm supposed to be on complete chair rest. Either in the bed or in the chair were my orders. They told me not to leave out of this room. When word got out that I could no longer leave my room to go and pray for the other patients, the nurses started sending them to me. God continued to bless! Nurses and other hospital staff have been coming in for prayer for various conditions and situations. God is richly blessing all of us. I promised the doctors and nurses that I would be good. I understood why I had been exiled to my room. In spite of this God still provided a way for me to minister to others. Rather than me going to them, God sent them to me. Whatever situation you are in and whatever troubles you might be experiencing, you still should take advantage of the opportunity to praise God, in good times and in bad times. David said in **Psalms 34:1**

"I will bless the Lord at all times: his praise shall continually be in my mouth."

It is now 5:20 A.M. Dr. Chris Adams just left and gave me a briefing on my condition. He stated that we are on the right track. My muscle enzyme level dropped about 300 points from the last time. It is now around 4,200 points. This is great news from having been over 30,000 on December 30, 1994. PRAISE BE TO GOD! So, the revival continues both day and night. I'm expecting God to do great things today!

I've had a great day today. God has really been blessing me today. I can feel that my departure is at hand but not just yet. There are still a few more assignments that God has for me to do in room 2344, St. Vincent Medical Center, in Little Rock, Arkansas.

God is yet blessing on day 28 of the soul saving, healing and deliverance revival. Many, including me, have been blessed as a result of God allowing me to be afflicted with this rare muscle disease. The sick has been healed, the lost has been saved, the lame is now walking, the blind is now seeing, the deaf is now hearing and the dead has now come alive. Many who were blind to the things that are of God can now see and those that were deaf to the Word of God can now hear. Many who were lame in the spirit can now walk and many who were walking around spiritually dead have now come alive. I am convinced more than ever what the Bible tells us **in Romans 8:28:**

"And we know that all things work together for good to them that love God, to them who are the called according to his purpose."

Being sick and being in the hospital has been a great blessing that God has allowed me to have, it has truly worked together for good! **Romans 8:31** says,

"What shall we then say to these things? If God be for us, who can be against us?"

I know that God is on my side! **Romans 8:37-39** tells us:

(37) "Nay, in all these things we are more than conquerors through him that loved us. (38) For I am

90

persuaded, that neither death, nor life, nor angels, nor principalities, nor powers, nor things present, nor things to come, (39) Nor height, nor depth, nor any other creature, shall be able to separate us from the love of God, which is in Christ Jesus our Lord."

The news about the man of God in room 2344 has been spread abroad. A doctor who is on staff here at St. Vincent heard that I was here and was impressed to come by to meet me. While he was here, we exchanged words of wisdom and then he related to me a quote by George Bernard Shaw that says:

"I'd rather believe in heaven and be disappointed than to be in the company and presence of those who did not believe."

That really touched my heart!
For the Bible says in **Revelation 21:8,**

"But the fearful, and unbelieving, and the abominable, and murderers and whoremongers, and sorcerers, and idolaters, and all liars, shall have their part in the lake which burneth with fire and brimstone: which is the second death."

Well, many great things have happened since I've been in room 2344. It's been a great experience, one that I will never forget. It's been heaven on earth, in spite of the circumstances. I'm reminded of a quote which says,

"Circumstances do not make a man; they just reveal what he is made of."

Another says,

"You don't drown by falling into the water, you only drown if you stay there,"

and another says,

"God does not allow us to go into deep waters to drown us, but so that we may learn to swim."

Through this ordeal, God has taught me how to swim through some very turbulent and some very tempestuous waters!

Many of my doctors have started pulling off of my case because of the miraculous recovery that God has given me. They have never seen anything quite like this recovery from the condition of dermatomyositis, but God is so great that no one will ever be able to understand his magnificence. How great thou art! What a friend we have in Jesus!

I've had from five to eight doctors working on my case to monitor my condition and the medications that I'm on. But there has only been one doctor who has monitored everything. His name is Dr. Jesus. Praise God! My other doctors have taken their orders from Him because I've had a great team of Christian doctors who have acknowledged the fact that God is in control of their medical practice and that their steps are ordered by Him. The Bible says in **Psalms** 37:23 that,

> *"The steps of a good man are ordered by the Lord: and he delighteth in his way."*

Day 28 has been great! I retired early tonight, around 10:00 P.M. I don't think that I will be doing a midnight revival tonight but I'm leaving my options open. You never, never know!

Good night and stay tuned for miracles that God will work on Friday, January 27, 1995.

Friday, January 27, 1995

It is now 4:20 A.M.; I have awakened and gotten out of bed to get cleaned up. My doctors should be here around 5:00 A.M. for my daily briefing concerning my condition.

5:05 A.M. has arrived and Dr. Chris Adams is proceeding to brief me concerning my condition. He is well pleased at my progress! He came in smiling and told me that my muscle enzyme level is down from over 30,000 points when I arrived on December 30, 1994 to around 3,500 on today, Friday, January 29, 1995. He states that when it gets below 3,000 I should be ready to go home and finish recuperating at home.

The normal enzyme level is around 250 points or below, so I still have a little ways to go but God has been faithful. I asked Dr.

Adams if he was trying to shut my revival down. I told him I needed a few more days in the hospital because I have some unfinished business to take care of and that I wasn't quite ready to end the revival. He looked at me kind of strangely and said "Okay, you can have a few more days." Praise God for that!

The revival that started on my first night in the hospital, December 30, 1994, is rapidly nearing a close. Sadness engulfs me knowing that the great time I've had in the hospital is nearing an end. The doctors, nurses, and the staff of St. Vincent have been great and have provided wonderful service and care to me. They will always be a part of me wherever I go. I cannot ever forget their kindness and I cannot thank God enough for allowing me to go through all the things I've gone through, for God did not allow it to happen to me to make me bitter, but to make me better.

God has been proving himself in my life and in the lives of others. The staff has advised me that my name and what God has done for me has been buzzing all over the hospital and has been spread abroad. I've also had the opportunity to share my testimony from my hospital bed on radio station KLRG 1150 on Thursday night, January 12, 1995 on the broadcast of my good friend, Elder Paul Robinson. I am also scheduled to give my testimony on radio station KITA 1440 on Saturday, January 28, 1995 on the broadcast of my good friends Elder and Sister Jerry Bradden. Praise God! God is just working so many good things out of this affliction. I share what David said in **Psalms 119:71:**

"It is good for me that I have been afflicted; that I might learn thy statutes"

"ALL IS WELL"!

Romans 8:18 says,

"For I reckon that the sufferings of this present time are not worthy to be compared with the glory which shall be revealed in us."

II **Timothy 2:12,**

"If we suffer, we shall also reign with him: If we deny him, he also will deny us:"

93

II **Timothy 3:12,**

"Yea, and all that will live godly in Christ Jesus shall suffer persecution."

I **Peter 3:17,**

"For it is better, if the will of God be so, that ye suffer for well doing, than for evil doing."

I **Peter 4:1,**

"Forasmuch then as Christ hath suffered for us in the flesh, arm yourselves likewise with the same mind: for he that hath suffered in the flesh hath ceased from sin";

I **Peter 4:12 through 16:**

(12) "Beloved, think it not strange concerning the fiery trial which is to try you, as though some strange thing happened unto you":

(13) "But rejoice, inasmuch as ye are partakers of Christ's sufferings; that, when his glory shall be revealed, ye may be glad also with exceeding joy".

(14) "If ye be reproached for the name of Christ, happy are ye; for the spirit of glory and of God resteth upon you: on their part he is evil spoken of, but on your part he is glorified".

(15) "But let none of you suffer as a murderer, or as a thief, or as an evildoer, or as a busybody in other men's matters".

(16) "Yet if any man suffer as a Christian, let him not be ashamed; but let him glorify God on this behalf".

II **Timothy** 2:3 says,

"Thou therefore endure hardness, as a good soldier of Jesus Christ."

James 1:2-4:

(2) "My brethren, count it all joy when ye fall into divers temptations";

(3) "Knowing this, that the trying of your faith worketh patience".

(4) "But let patience have her perfect work, that ye may be perfect and entire, wanting nothing".

One of my doctors, Dr. Raymond Miller, arrived at 6:00 A.M. and was pleased with my progress and stated that he has only seen two people in his 25 years of medical practice with the disease that I have and neither one of them rebounded from it as I have. PRAISE THE LORD!

Today will be a great day and "ALL IS WELL!"

Three employees from the hospital came in for morning prayer around 7:00 A.M. this morning. God really poured out his spirit on them and they left the room rejoicing and praising God. Praise be to God! He is faithful! Stay tuned for more great things that will happen today.

I'm expecting my wonderful daughter, Eboni, to spend the night with me at the hospital tonight. Eboni has been faithful to call me around 6:25 A.M. each morning to check on me and to see how I am doing.

This looks like my final weekend in room 2344, St. Vincent Medical Center, in Little Rock, Arkansas. It's been great but all good things must come to an end!

Eboni arrived around 6:30 P.M. We had a great time tonight. She is excited about getting to spend the night with her daddy. We watched part of a Gospel Videotape. We stayed up late and talked and had lots of fun. She is thirteen years old and is an eighth grade student at Mabelvale Junior High School in Little Rock.

Saturday January 28, 1995
This is day 30 of my wonderful stay here at St. Vincent Infirmary Medical Center, room 2344.

It has been a great day! Eboni and I have had a great time today. We slept late and then got up and ate breakfast together. We received the wrong tray for breakfast, but they more than made up for it after I called the kitchen and explained my dilemma. They gladly brought up another tray. I had ordered some extra breakfast because I knew that Eboni would be with me. They really took good care of us. They sent about eight pancakes, eight strips of bacon, scrambled eggs, hot grits, Raisin Bran, toast, jelly, milk, juice and all the trimmings. God really blessed us at breakfast time. He poured out a blessing that we didn't have room to receive!

Well, after that big breakfast, Eboni and I got sleepy again and took a nap. We got up and took a few phone calls and then it was time for me to call in to Elder and Sister Jerry Bradden's radio broadcast to give a live testimony of what God is doing for me in St. Vincent Hospital, room 2344. It went just great. We taped the testimony as I gave it over the air. We have been listening to a copy of the tape over and over. Eboni said I did a great job! I was proud to hear that coming from a child. Next, we tried to clean up our room.

Then it was lunch time and we shared a great lunch together. After lunch, we tried to clean up again. After finally getting things cleaned up, Eboni made a sign to go on my wall that said "Number One Dad in the World." I certainly did appreciate that. She displayed it on the wall for all to see. After that, my brother James Johnson came with some goodies and candy for the candy jar that I kept as a positive reinforcer for my nursing staff and visitors. God has blessed me to have the greatest doctors and the greatest nursing staff on earth at St. Vincent Hospital. They have been overwhelmingly wonderful to me and my family!

It is now 5:30 P.M. My lovely wife Marie arrives for a visit and to pick up Eboni. Eboni is in no way ready to go. She has had a great time being here at the hospital with her dad. It is now about 6:10 P.M., Pastor Jewel Withers Jr., who has been so faithful in visiting me, has arrived to check on me. Around 8:00 P.M. my neighbors Raymond and Jennie Van Buren arrived to check on me. After hearing me on the radio earlier today, Jennie Van Buren called the hospital and expressed how much she enjoyed me on the radio. She expressed that she had no idea that I was in the hospital. It was great to see them and "ALL IS WELL!" My neighbor Bert Presson also called to check on me.

It is now 11:20 P.M. I just called home to see if my son Eric and his cousin Samuel Jordan had arrived home from bowling. They haven't arrived yet. I won't be able to sleep until they do. Nurses Margaret Washington and Joyce Larry were my wonderful nurses for tonight. They helped to put my mind at ease.

This is all for now. I must get some rest, who knows, I may have to do a midnight revival!

Sunday, January 29, 1995

Eric and Sam made it in fine last night. Thanks be to God!

Day 31 has been a great day! I got a chance to rest this morning.

About 3:00 P.M. today, I got a great surprise. My brother Charles Johnson from Detroit, Michigan, surprised me as he walked in my room. He has called me about 100 times from Detroit since I've been in the hospital. He had called me about 7:00 A.M. this morning to see how I was doing. When he got ready to hang up, he told me that he would talk to me later on today. He showed up in my room at 3:00 P.M. I was so happy to see him. I found out later that when he called me at 7:00 A.M., he was at the Detroit Airport preparing to come to Little Rock to see me. He gave no indication at all that he was on his way. It was a great surprise!

This was the day of the Super Bowl and my wonderful son Eric spent the entire day with me. We had a great time together. I also had visitors from my home church today, Mother Fannie Bullocks who is close to 90 years old and Sister Earline Tolbert, Sister Mary Grayer and Pastor Jewel Withers, Jr. I was also richly blessed today by having my wonderful mother, Mrs. Laura Johnson to come to visit me. Many other family members came today. My brother James Johnson and his wife Ozetta, my lovely wife Marie and my daughter Eboni, my brother Clint Johnson and his wife Sharon, my niece Trese Johnson and her daughter Brooklyn.

Co-workers from the Conway Human Development Center, Lisa Koch, Marilyn Colclasure, Carolyn Wade and Regina Peterman also came to visit me today.

Today has been an especially wonderful day for me! Again my wonderful son Eric got to spend the entire day with me. He is to be highly commended because he has done such an outstanding job in being the man around the house while I have been ill and in the hospital. He has done a great job in helping to take care of his mother and his sister, I am so proud of him! He is 17 years old and is a senior at J.A. Fair High School in Little Rock. He hasn't been able to spend the night with me because I didn't want my wife and daughter left at home alone. He has certainly done more than his part in helping me through this entire ordeal. My illness has taken a great toll on him though. He has been very concerned as to whether I will recover from this devastating illness. I have tried to assure him that "ALL IS WELL!" He has watched me deteriorate from being very active to being where I can barely do anything for myself. It really helped him to get to spend the day with me and he was very happy to do so.

He has been a lot of help to me today. We got a chance to talk about my illness and I let him know that there is nothing too hard for God and that I felt that I would be completely healed of this disease. Knowing that I am very optimistic about my full recovery really helped to put his mind at ease. The nurses really didn't have to come in as much today because Eric took great care of me! I am still in a very feeble and weakened condition but God is blessing me to make progress. I have come a long way and have a long way to go, but I am very optimistic about the future!

What helped to make this an especially great day for Eric and me is that we got to watch the Super Bowl together. I was so happy that we got to spend some time together. When it came time for him to go, I graciously thanked him for taking time out to spend the day with me. I gave him a fatherly talk and told him not to worry about me, because "ALL IS WELL!"

With my brother Charles coming to town today, we have had a great family reunion right here in my hospital room. All of us really enjoyed his visit. He told me that throughout my illness, I had been telling him on the telephone that "ALL IS WELL" but he felt like he needed to come see for himself. He quickly found out that my body may be weak but my spirit is strong. I realize that the "outlook may be dark but the uplook is bright." David said in Psalms 121: verses 1-2.

(1) "I will lift up mine eyes unto the hills, from whence cometh my help".

(2) "My help cometh from the Lord, which made heaven and earth."

This is certainly where my help is coming from! Charles and I had a great night. We stayed up late and talked about old times.

Monday, January 30, 1995

It is 4:00 A.M. Charles and Roy awakens and begins a discussion of several issues concerning our childhood days. This session was tape recorded. I thought I was taping it secretly but when it was over Charles said he knew I was taping it. We both got a kick out of it.

At 5:45 A.M. one of my doctors, Dr. Raymond Miller, came in and Charles got to meet him and he discussed my condition with him.

At 6:30 A.M. Dr. Christopher Adams arrived. Charles also got to meet him and discussed my condition with him.

7:00 A.M. Charles and Roy are still sleepy from the 4:00 A.M. dialogue. Charles goes back to sleep. Roy has to get up and get cleaned up so I can eat breakfast before I go to physical therapy. Willie Johnson, who works in the physical therapy department, will be here soon to transport me to therapy and he wants me to be ready.

8:00 A.M. some good friends of mine, Reverend and Mrs. David Gober, arrive. I enjoyed their visit greatly. Charles met them also.

At 9:15 A.M. Willie Johnson arrives. Charles gets up to get cleaned up. My sister-in-law Sharon Johnson will pick him up at 11:00 A.M. to transport him to the Little Rock National Airport for a 12 noon flight back to Detroit, Michigan. I arrived back from physical therapy at approximately 10:40 A.M., l got back in time to say goodbye to Charles. I really enjoyed his visit with me at the hospital. He never left the hospital from the time he arrived at 3:00 P.M., Sunday, January 29th. This visit was especially for me!

Today I received a wonderful visit from my dad, Elder William Johnson, who is 86 years old, and his wife Ms. Rose. I also received visits from family members Clint Johnson and Willie and Earnestine Montgomery. I received visits from friends and co-workers Dr. James Pinkerton and his wife Betty, Jackie Young, Evada Thomas, Freida Marsh, Estella Forte, Marie Mahan, Johnny Shadell, Al Lambert, Iola Donaldson and many others. God has blessed me with so many visits from so many wonderful people.

God bless and stay tuned!

Tuesday, January 31, 1995

It's 3:30 A.M. on day 33. I woke up and began praising God for His goodness and loving kindness and tender mercy. After praising God, I went back to sleep.

This is the first time that I have really felt like my old self again. God has been great to me. He has brought me from a mighty long way!!!

One of the nurses told me that several of them were of the opinion that I would not live through the night when I entered the hospital on December 30, 1994. They knew that I was a very, very, sick man, but God is faithful! I told them that if I live it is well, and if I die it is well. I let then know that if I should die I will praise God on the other side, and if I should live I will keep on praising Him over here!

6:00 A.M. Dr. Christopher Adams arrived and gave me the good news that I will get to go home on Thursday, February 2, 1995, if things continue to go well. My muscle enzyme level is down to around 3,000 from having been over 30,000 on

December 30, 1994. PRAISE GOD! The normal range is around 250 points or below. I am on my way!!!

The doctor had mentioned to me last week that this may be the week that I get to go home but I advised him that I was not ready to close out the red hot revival that has been going on in my room. I told him that I needed a few more days to complete the assignment that God had sent me in here to do.

He said that he understood and he extended my stay for a few extra days until my assignment was completed. PRAISE GOD! At this point I am still very weak but we thought that this would be a good time to see if I would be able to do well at home.

Thursday, February 2, 1995 will be day 35!!!

This has been a great day! I have been taking pictures of everybody. It's been a great day!!!

The T.V. lady, Ms. Jean Butler, came by to collect for the T.V. today. Upon being advised that Thursday would be my last day, she immediately stated that she wanted to donate two days of free T.V. to me. She stated that I had been a great blessing to her as she came in and out of my room. PRAISE GOD! Another T.V. lady who was exceptionally nice to me was Lorene Chandler. Lorene is also a nurse here at the hospital.

At 4:00 A.M. on this day when I got back in bed I was able to turn on my side and sleep for the first time in two and a half months. I've had to sleep on my back for the last two and a half months because I didn't have the strength to turn over.

Today I received a wonderful visit from my sister-in-law Dr. Joanna Edwards. She has really been by my side through my illness. I also received visits from friends and co-workers, Eula West, Ms. Kelly, Perry and Carolyn Pratt, Darlene Owens, Reverend Wesley Townsend and his wife Annie, Reverend Robert Townsend and his wife Karen, Frank Jackson, Diane Lucas and her sister, Debbie Pruitt, Stella Lowe and many other friends and relatives. I also received many wonderful and encouraging calls from my sister-in-law Kathy Johnson during my stay here in the hospital. I have also received some very encouraging calls from my sister-in-law Peggy Johnson.

Wednesday, February 1, 1995

Praise the Lord! Today is February 1, 1995. Another midnight revival occurred last night. God really blessed!

My time is at hand. I've got today, Wednesday, February 1st, and then Thursday, February 2nd. The revival in room 2344 ends as far as the principal evangelist is concerned, but God raised up other evangelists here in the hospital who will continue the spirit and motivation that God has endowed us with at St. Vincent Hospital and Room 2344 will never be the same again!

Dr. Christopher Adams arrived at approximately 5:45 A.M. and confirmed again my going home on Thursday. Today has been a great day, but I will truly miss the wonderful doctors, nurses, and the entire staff of St. Vincent Hospital. They have been super wonderful!

The time has come for me to return to my lovely family, who have been so wonderful to me during my illness and my hospital stay.

My wife Marie is to be commended. She has done an outstanding job of keeping everything going at home. By the way, she has commented that more money seems to be in the checkbook since I have been sick. One reason is that I have not had the strength to make it to Wal-Mart, my favorite store.

The children have been great to check on me and to help keep things going. Eric is to be commended for helping to take care of his mother and sister and for being the man around the house while I've been gone.

Eboni has been great! She calls me every morning around 6:25 A.M. to say "good morning" and to see how my night went.

RETURNED HOME FROM HOSPITAL

Thursday, February 2, 1995

Today, Thursday, February 2, 1995, is the 35th day of my hospital stay. It really doesn't seem like 35 days because this has been heaven on earth. God didn't allow this rare disease of the muscles to come upon me to make me bitter but to make me better. You have a choice: You can become bitter, or you can become better. I chose to become better! I have received over 400 telephone calls, and over 300 get well cards, letters, and notes, and other gestures of love during the 35 days of my hospital stay. I have gotten calls from all over the state of Arkansas and from places such as Atlanta, Los Angeles, Dallas, and Chicago; and over 100 phone calls from my brother Charles in Detroit, MI. My brother Samuel and his wife, Nell have called over 10 times from Verona, Italy, where she is stationed with the U.S. Army.

Everyone has been so great! The nursing staff has been simply outstanding! I haven't wanted for anything. They have treated me better than a king would have been treated. Employees from work have been overwhelmingly wonderful! Mr. Bob Clark, Superintendent of the Conway Human Development Center where I work and Mrs. Carol Shockley, the Assistant Superintendent, and their staff have been absolutely wonderful to me. Mr. Ed Jennings, my supervisor, has gone above and beyond the call of duty to assist me in whatever I needed. My co-workers in Staff Development have taken over my workload for me. Alesia Holbrook and her Dietetic Staff, Joyce Rossi, Kaye Malcom and Robin Steinmetz have combined with Staff Development to call me everyday to cheer me up. My secretary, Shirley Crawford, is in charge of calling me. Other members of Staff Development who have also been so kind to me are Mary Jane Russell, Sharon Mohammed, Linda Henderson, and the personnel staff, which included Carolyn Coney, Linda Parker, Dottie Dominguez, Jennifer Ingram, Laura Stockenbury, Terry Clifton and the entire CHDC staff!

It's been a wonderful experience being in the hospital. Many other employees from the Center have called and come by to express their concern.

My wife and family have been truly outstanding! They have really been very supportive of me during my illness. I've never been away from them for 35 days before. While in the hospital, I got to be on two radio stations giving my testimony from my hospital bed. God has truly blessed me and others have been blessed as a result of my being here.

Day 35 started around 4:30 A.M., I got up, cleaned up, ate breakfast, and began to pack up all my belongings for the trip home. At approximately 9:00 A.M. I went to physical therapy and was briefed on what I should do when I get home. I arrived back in my room around 10:30 A.M. I was visited by the social work staff who advised me of some matters that I need to be aware of. At approximately 11:00 A.M. today I received a call from the St. Vincent Communications office. They would like to interview me before I leave the hospital today. They want to put a picture of me, and a write-up about my stay in the hospital in their monthly newsletter.

Earlier this morning I called many of the St. Vincent nurses and staff into my room and personally thanked them for their kindness to me and my family over the last 35 days. I expressed to them that I had been truly blessed by the love that they had shown me and the very compassionate care that they had given me. I let them know that my departure was at hand but I didn't want the revival to stop simply because I was leaving. I encouraged them to keep the revival going and to continue to love one another. I then laid hands on each of them and prayed God's blessings upon them that they would continue to be a blessing to others as they have been to me. I told them that each one of them was being held personally responsible for keeping the revival going. I will truly miss each one of them. As we parted, we bade each other Godspeed and we vowed to always keep in touch.

At approximately 11:45 A.M. Mr. John Patton from St. Vincent Communications Office arrived to interview me. The interview lasted approximately 45 minutes. At 12:30 P.M. lunch arrived. I ate lunch, packed a few more things, and laid down around 1:15 P.M. to rest from the very hectic morning.

At 1:45 P.M. my wife arrives to help me pack some things so that I can go home. Around 2:00 P.M. about ten nurses just arrived to help load all of my flowers and belongings onto about 5 carts. At 2:15 P.M. I looked at the staff and heard them saying goodbye and best wishes for a speedy recovery. Upon seeing the sadness on their faces, I began to cry and I reminisced over the kindness that they had shown me and my family for the last 35 days. They also had become family for me and it was difficult to accept the fact that this was coming to an end. Again, I sincerely thanked them for the wonderful care that they had given me for the last 35 days.

At 2:45 P.M., I departed from St. Vincent Infirmary Medical Center en route to my home. There were a few stops that my wife and I needed to make. I finally arrived home about 4:00 P.M. after having been gone for 35 days. It's great to be home! Everything looks different!

At the hospital tears were shed when they were saying goodbye to me and I looked at the empty room, but when I got home smiles were there and they were saying hello to me. So the tears shed when I left the hospital were turned to smiles of joy when I arrived home on February 2, 1995. After being gone for 35 days everything looked different. The rooms looked larger, surroundings looked different. I finally got adjusted and after awhile everything was back to normal. I was so glad to be united back with my family.

Around 4:15 P.M. Taylor Home Health arrived with a wheelchair for me to use. Around 4:30 P.M. my wonderful son Eric arrived home from school. It was so great to see him! I thanked him for helping to take care of his mother and sister while I was gone. We were so glad to see each other.

About 5:15 P.M. my lovely daughter Eboni arrived home. We were so glad to see each other. She was so happy that her daddy was back home. Sister Rose Pryor and her daughter Vickie James came by around 7:00 P.M. to see me at home. Sister Pryor had gone to the hospital to see me but was told I had been discharged. She later came by my house along with Vickie. We had a great time!

Friday, February 3, 1995

At Home!

I'm home! I'm home!

I slept in my own bed last night! It's great to be home after 35 days. Although I had a great time at the hospital, "There is no place like home!"

Today has been a great day for me. I got up around 6:30 A.M. to help get my family ready and to see them off to school and work. My wife helped me around the house before she went to work.

Around 8:15 A.M. Taylor Home Health arrived to bring equipment to put in the bathtub to make it easier for me to take a shower. This is my dad's birthday. He is 87 years old today. I called and wished him a happy birthday. He is so glad that I am back home. He was really worried about me.

Friday night went great!

Saturday, February 4, 1995

AT HOME

Saturday went great! I got up around 8:00 A.M., to get ready for the physical therapist to come. I got up, thanked God for another day, shaved, cut my hair, showered, and ate breakfast. At 9:30 A.M. my physical therapist arrived to begin my physical therapy program.

Saturday was a real restful day. My brother James and my niece Brook came by to see me. My mother called and I received a few other calls. God has really blessed me today. I can do things today that I was not able to do yesterday. At about 4:00 P.M. I received a call from my nurses at St. Vincent. Joyce Larry, Margaret Washington, and Peg Lufkin called me. They advised me that after I went home Thursday, everyone came in and was very sad to know that I had been discharged. They also told me that another patient had been moved to my room.

They also told me that the strangest thing happened between 12 midnight and 1:00 A.M. last night. About this time the nurses' button automatically went off and it was ringing at the nurses' station. I had just been discharged Thursday about 2:15 P.M. Had I still been in room 2344 this would have been the time that I probably would have been in the midst of my midnight revival service. The lady in the room stated that she did not press the button but when she tried to shut it off, it would not shut off.

The staff was shook up and didn't know what to do. They could not get the device to stop ringing. The lady in the room could not rest because of it. They finally had to call maintenance about 1:30 A.M. to change the entire system out.

The staff and I concluded that I had just ended 35 days of revival services in room 2344 in the flesh and that my spirit stepped back in the room for one more "midnight revival service." So, even though I'm physically gone from the hospital God allows His spirit to continue to dwell at St. Vincent Hospital and especially in room 2344, the room that was sanctified and made holy by the power of God. The room that the man of God called home for 35 days. PRAISE GOD!

At approximately 5:30 P.M., after talking with my nurses, I pondered over what good thing that I could do for them to show my appreciation for all that they had done for me. I concluded that since I had supplied them with Snickers and Starburst candies while in room 2344, I felt that this would be a very welcomed gesture. The candy is what helped to keep them going.

I called my pastor, Pastor Jewel Withers, Jr., who had been asking me during the last 35 days if there was anything that he could do for me. I finally gave him the chance to do a very important thing for me; I asked if he would deliver a bag of Snickers and a bag of Starburst Candies to my nurses on 3NW, St. Vincent Hospital. He happily agreed to do this for me. I was so grateful!

At 9:30 P.M. Pastor Withers called and told me that the mission was completed and everyone was happy to know that I was thinking about them enough to have someone to "special deliver" a special treat to them that they really loved and that they had gotten accustomed to for 35 days. At 10:00 P.M. St. Vincent nurses Joyce Larry and Margaret Washington called to thank me for the treats. They were so happy!

PRAISE GOD!

Sunday, February 5, 1995

AT HOME

Sunday went great! My wife and children went to church. We had a great time when they returned.

They went back to church Sunday night. Eboni was winner of the Youth Bible Talent Contest. She came home really excited!

Monday, February 6, 1995

AT HOME

Monday went great! A nurse from St. Vincent Home Health Office came by the house around 11:30 A.M. She checked my blood pressure and had me to complete some paper work.

At 1:30 P.M. my physical therapist arrived to do physical therapy. I refused to do my therapy until I was able to contact my doctor, which took about twenty minutes. I realized from the first visit with the therapist that probably a little too much therapy was attempted than I was physically ready for. I had asked the therapist to call my doctor before returning so that they could talk about my limitations. He did not. But before doing any therapy today we talked to the doctor.

The issue was that my doctor had told me that my therapy was to be very limited because of my weakened condition. The therapist seemed to be wanting to get me well with therapy all in one day. I told him that Rome was not built in a day and that it would take time to get me back where I was before I got sick. My doctor talked with the therapist and we concurred that therapy should proceed at a slow rate and then build from there. We then got on the same page of the same book and I proceeded to allow the therapist to go on with therapy. The day ended with everyone happy!

My therapy was completed for February 6, 1995. The therapist should return on Thursday, February 8th at 1:30 P.M. The rest of the day went great! Physical therapy should continue until the end of April, 1995.

Tuesday, February 7, 1995

Today went great! Again it is so great to be back home with my family. I am still very weak and fragile but I know in due time God will raise me up where I belong. I will keep the faith in spite of my circumstances, and regardless of how long it takes. My day started around 5:30 A.M. I'm still accustomed to getting up around this time from being in the hospital. This would be the time that the lab employees would come around to draw blood samples and the time when I would be briefed by Dr. Christopher Adams and Dr. Raymond Miller on the progress of my condition.

Physical therapy went well yesterday. I was given some therapy exercises to do each day in addition to the ones that I do on the days when my therapist is here. I've got a great therapist! His name is Mike Kumpuris. He will be coming to do therapy with me twice a week. I did my therapy exercises around 7:00 A.M. I also helped to get my wife and children ready for school and work. Day 40 was spent praising God for how he is blessing me to be alive and back home with my family. My wife and children have been truly wonderful and outstanding. I am having to adjust to being here alone, but "ALL IS WELL!"

It has been less than a week since I've come home from the hospital and I truly miss the nurses and the many friends that I made there. The nurses have called me several times to let me know how much they miss me. I have also called them several times at midnight, at 3:00 A.M. in the morning and at other times during the day so that I can keep in touch with the various shifts. I will never forget the kindness that everyone has shown to me.

I am able to stay alone and take care of myself during the day while my wife is at work and my children are at school. I look forward to seeing them each evening. Eboni goes to Mablevale Jr. High School. She is picked up each day at 4:00 P.M. by Ms. Gwen Wise and her mother Mrs. Laverne Smith. They have taken care of Eboni since she was a baby. My wife picks her up around

5:00 P.M. from their house. Ms. Laverne, Gwen, Glenda, Mr. Bodie and the entire Smith family have been extremely kind to us over the years in providing care for both Eric and Eboni. We are deeply grateful to them for that!

As I mentioned, I am able to take care of myself here at home. While I was in the hospital, the physical therapists did a great job of teaching me how to walk again, how to use my hands again and how to become a fully functioning individual again. Therapist Mary Beth McDonald, Stephanie Mohr, Karen James, Carla Lowry and the entire physical therapy staff are to be commended for the outstanding job that they do for St. Vincent Infirmary Medical Center. They really devoted a lot of time and effort in helping me to recover from my illness. I praise God for them! The techniques of ambulation and mobility that the therapist taught me in the hospital really helped me at home. I normally do my therapy on the floor of the living room. Since I am in such a weakened condition I have to crawl over to the couch and pull up on it like a baby in order to get back on my feet. I also have a wheelchair to use to prevent me from being on my feet too much, but "ALL IS WELL!"

OBSERVATIONS FROM FEBRUARY 1995 TO FEBRUARY 1997

God blessed me to make many significant accomplishments during this time period. My physical therapy continues twice a week. I had a follow-up doctor visit on February 16th, 1995 with Dr. Christopher Adams. I am progressing well since my discharge from the hospital. My muscle enzyme level is down to 1700. I thank God for the progress that I am making. He has brought me from a mighty long way!

I visited Dr. Joe Pevahouse, Kidney Specialist on March 1st for a follow-up visit. All was well. I also had a doctor visit today with Dr. Guy Gardner, Ear, Nose and Throat Specialist. During my illness I have had problems with my throat and serious swallowing difficulties. Dr. Gardner examined me and prescribed some medication that should help in alleviating the problem. On March 7th I had a follow-up visit with my family physician, Internal Medicine Specialist, Dr. Raymond Miller. Everything is coming along just fine and he is very pleased with my progress. On March 16th, I had another check-up with my Rheumatologist, Dr. Christopher Adams. My muscle enzyme level at this time is 398. PRAISE GOD! God is truly blessing me and is giving me a speedy recovery. Dr. Adams is very pleased with my progress. My strength is getting better but I still have a long way to go, but by the help of God I will get there. During this visit I discussed with Dr. Adams the possibility of me trying to drive again. The last time that I drove was around December 22, 1994, when at such time I became too weak to drive. He questioned me thoroughly about my mental and physical ability to handle driving a vehicle again. I assured him that "ALL IS WELL!" He gave me permission to gradually get back into the driving routine. I assured him that I would exercise extreme caution. I felt that in order for me to get back to normal again, I would have to put forth some extra effort on my part. I was still very weak but I knew that with God's help I could do it!

March 16th and 17th was spent with my children Eboni and Eric. They were out of school for teacher workdays. They will be out for Spring break, March 20-24th. We had a great time together!

On March 20, 1995, I convinced my wife, Marie, and my daughter Eboni that it was time for me to make an attempt at driving again. They also questioned me as Dr. Adams did as to whether I felt like I was really able to handle it right now. Eric was not at home at the time, so I only had two people that I had to convince. I assured them that "all is well"! My next task was to convince them that it would be safe for them to ride with me, since they were afraid for me to go out alone and they were afraid to go with me. Around 5:30 P.M. today, I succeeded in convincing them that it was time to give me a chance to prove to them that I could still handle driving a vehicle. At 6:00 P.M. my wife and daughter assisted me out of the house and into the vehicle because I was still very weak, but I felt so very confident that it was time for me to drive again. As I sat behind the wheel, I must admit that it felt like the first time that I had ever gotten behind the wheel of a car. It felt very strange and I wondered what would be the outcome of this trip, yet I was convinced and determined to give it a try. I had to familiarize myself with the controls on the car again. When I felt comfortable with everything, I looked at my wife and daughter and told them that I was ready. I could see the great concern that was written over their faces. They let me know that they were riding with me only because they loved me and because they knew that if they didn't go with me that I was prepared to go alone and they certainly didn't want that with me being in the very weakened condition that I am in. Everyone fastened their seat belts and we were off! We drove around the city of Little Rock for awhile and then returned home. When we returned we all were convinced that I still had it! They praised me on how well I did after having been away from driving for three months and after having been through such a life-threatening disease of the muscles. I was very proud of myself and I praised God for allowing things to work out so well. It was quite an adjustment, but another milestone had been accomplished.

During this time I was still on some very potent medication that caused my appearance to change drastically. I gained a lot of weight; my facial features were very disfigured and distorted. It was very difficult for me to venture out of the house and face the public because I was very self-conscious as to how I looked. I would always have to tell people who I was and what had happened to me. God blessed me and the more I went out the better I felt. I knew that my facial features would get back to normal as my medication was decreased and then I would eventually be taken off of it. I learned a lot by being in this condition and it allows me to relate to what other people feel when they are experiencing similar situations in life.

On March 21, 1995, my wife's father, Mr. Wilmer Page, Sr. from Rosston, Arkansas came and spent the night with us and the next day he painted the inside of our house for us. I was deeply grateful to him for doing this. He did a great job and we had a great time together. Everything looks so beautiful!

Eric and Eboni were out on spring break and assisted him some but all I was able to do was to supervise. March continued to go well and my strength is gradually returning. At my last visit to Dr. Christopher Adams on March 16th, I asked him when he thought that I would be able to return to work. He stated that I had made significant progress but my physical condition had not improved enough to make a decision at this time. He said that we will talk about it again at my next visit on April 16th. Much of the decision will depend on how much progress I make over the next month. I feel mentally capable but not physically able at this point. I feel like I will make significant progress over the next month. God is able!

A very humorous thing happened on Wednesday, March 29th. I hobbled out to the mailbox to check the mail. After getting the mail, I proceeded to go back in the house. As I opened the screen door, the front door automatically closed. As I reached for the doorknob, I quickly realized that I was locked out of the house without a key. It was windy, sunny and mild. Thank God it was not cold! After realizing that I was locked out of the house with only a tee shirt and pajamas and a long black overcoat on, I sat down on the front porch and pondered how I would get back into the house. I did happen to have a portable phone with me but I hated to call my wife at work and tell her that I was locked out of the house. I was still very weak at this time and was basically helpless. I sat on the porch for about 30 minutes waving and smiling at my neighbors and others who passed by. I didn't want my neighbors to know that I was locked out so I acted as though I was just out there getting some fresh air. I called my wife and asked her if she would come home from work to let me in the house. She did and I learned a lot that day and I never went out again without my keys and the telephone. "ALL IS WELL"!

My days have been spent praying, reading my Bible, doing my physical therapy, and eating up everything in sight because the medicine that I am on has given me an enormous appetite. One day my wife brought home a chocolate cake from the store. The next evening they came home and were looking for some chocolate cake but it was gone. They tease me about that frequently. My days have also been spent taking phone calls from friends and family. I am home alone and I need to keep busy. I have also been answering letters and sending thank you cards to family and friends, thanking them for their many, many acts of kindness that they have shown me during my illness. Since I have been ill I have received over 500 get well cards and letters, over 500 phone calls, and over 500 visits from family and friends. I have also received many other warm expressions of love and concern from family and friends. Chaplain George Andrews from work came to see me the other day. We had a great visit. Many other employees came to see me while I was at home recuperating. Some of them were my supervisor Mr. Ed Jennings, Mary Jane Russell, Shirley Crawford, and Linda Henderson, who brought her class with her. This would be the group I would have had if I were at work. She and Sharon Mohammed took turns taking care of my classes for me. Other employees who taught classes for me during my illness were Darren Jeanneret, Ed Jennings, Judy Fite, Shelbie Huff and others.

On April 3rd I had a doctor visit with Dermatologist, Dr. Gregory Dwyer. I consulted with him for treatment of skin rashes on my face, hands, fingers and legs. This has been a result of the disease of dermatomyositis. There has also been noticeable skin discoloration on my face. I also had a follow-up visit with Kidney Specialist, Dr. Joe Pevahouse. All is well! During this time my sugar level went up to around 689. Some of it was caused by the medication and I think some was caused by my eating too much sweets. I was put on a strict diet and some medication. It was taken care of and again, "all is well". Eric is a senior at J.A. Fair High School here in Little Rock and is scheduled to graduate in May. I am still very disfigured from the medication and I am still in a very weakened condition. I still have difficulty getting in and out of a chair and getting in and out of bed, but God is continuing to bless me. I am using a wheelchair some so that I won't have to constantly be on my legs. I am still confident that God will completely deliver me in due time. Physical therapy continues to go well. My therapy is done on the living room floor. It's not too bad getting down on the floor; the main problem is getting up. I have to crawl over to the couch like a baby and pull up on the couch in order to get on my feet, but "ALL IS WELL". I am just so glad that I am still alive. God is giving me a testimony. I realize that "no test, no testimony". This is only a test!

During this time I received flowers from my good friends and co-workers Gary and Shirley Throckmorton. They came by way of Federal Express, sealed in a box that I refused to open for a couple of days because the only information that I had was that this box was from somewhere in California. Since there have been so many people who have been killed and injured by opening packages containing bombs, I immediately took the package to a secluded area in the garage and left it there unopened until I could hear from the person who may have sent it. About three days after I received the package, I got a call from Shirley Throckmorton. She talked for a few minutes waiting for me to acknowledge that I received their flowers. When I didn't, she asked me if I received any flowers from her and Gary. I suddenly realized that this was the package that I was afraid to open and had put in a secluded area of the garage. I asked her to hold on for a moment while I hurried to the garage, retrieved and opened the package and discovered some beautiful flowers with Gary's and Shirley's name on the inside. I picked up the phone and apologized to her and shared with her my concerns about opening it since their name was not on the outside. I immediately watered the flowers and placed them in a special place in the living room. They look so beautiful! Also during this time I was getting temporary handicapped parking stickers from the revenue office. By this time I had gotten about two stickers that were good for three months each. I had gone to the same person each time. She observed the severe physical condition that I was in and she very politely suggested that I might want to get a permanent handicapped license tag. I very politely thanked her for her genuine concern for me but I expressed to her that this was only a temporary illness and that God was in the process of working a miracle for me. She then completed the paperwork for a temporary sticker, smiled and wished me well. I thanked her again for her concern. Her name is Trichia.

Another great experience occurred on Sunday, April 16, 1995, Easter Sunday. This was the day that I was able to return to church after being out ill for the past five months. I had a great time. I got to give my testimony and everyone was glad to see me, although I looked a lot different from the last time they saw me. This was one of the side effects of the medication. This was a great day to return since Easter Sunday was the day that Jesus was resurrected from the dead and I was being resurrected from my sickbed.

On April 18th, I had another doctor visit with Dr. Christopher Adams. My check-up turned out really good. I am steadily making significant progress and my strength gradually returning. My muscle enzyme level at this time is at an all-time low of 72. At this visit I discussed with Dr. Adams again the possibility of me returning to work. He talked a little doubtful at first but I began to convince him of the great things that God was doing for me and the things

116

that he had in store for me. He stressed to me that if I did return to work that I would have to exercise extreme caution because he did not want me to have to experience again the severe illness that I am being delivered from. I told him that I understood and that I would take care of myself. We talked about several options concerning my reintegration into the workforce. Both of us agreed that we would gradually work back into a full schedule. He told me that I could return to work on Monday, May 8, 1995, if I am good. The first two weeks I would work half a day on Monday, Wednesday and Friday. For the third week, I would work half a day for five days. The fourth week I would return to a full 40-hour-a-week work schedule. I graciously thanked him for trusting my judgment on my assessment of my physical and mental readiness to return to work. Throughout my illness Dr. Adams has always valued my opinion and suggestions on issues concerning my illness. He has been an outstanding physician!

Wednesday, April 19, 1995, is a day that will forever be etched in my memory. I had been invited to lunch by a good friend of mine, Mr. J.J. Pace. Mr. Pace was coming by the house to pick me up so that we could go to Shoney's Restaurant, a few blocks from my house. While waiting for him to pick me up I was watching a television program that was interrupted by a special bulletin concerning the tragic Oklahoma City Federal Building bombing. I watched as people lay maimed and helpless and observed the devastation that the bomb had caused and listened as the death toll of men, women, boys and girls began to rise. My prayers immediately went out for the injured, their families, and for the families, of those who had lost loved ones. It was a day that I will never forget. Mr. Pace finally arrived and we went out to eat but we were subdued by the tragic happenings of the day.

Well, May 8th, 1995 is fastly approaching. This is the day that I am scheduled to return to work after being ill for the past five months. The word is out! I have advised many people that the time for my return to work is at hand. Many people were happy at the idea but some were still concerned about my physical ability to handle the task. I tried to convince them that "ALL

IS WELL." By the way, at this time I had been approved to receive Social Security disability benefits that would start coming in a few weeks. It was suggested that since I was still in a very weakened condition that I delay returning to work for awhile and receive the approved Social Security benefits in the meantime. I told them that I had heard from God and that it was time for me to return to work in spite of having been approved for Social Security benefits. I told them that one day I might need to receive Social Security disability benefits but not right now. I graciously thanked them for their genuine concern for me. Plans were made for me to forge on with the decision to return to work on May 8th. Everyone at work is anticipating my return. The word is out!

Monday, May 8th has finally arrived! The alarm clock went off around 4:30 A.M. I am excited about returning to the place and people that I dearly love and to the ones who have shown in such great ways their love and concern for me over the last year. I tell people frequently that I live in Little Rock and work in Conway, and the closer I get to work, the better I feel and sometimes I just pull up in the parking lot and jump out of my car and run to the building. I also tell them that every other Thursday when I get paid, I feel that I ought to be the one paying the state for allowing me to work there rather than the state paying me. It is a wonderful place to work and I feel that it would be good therapy for me to return at this time. There are so many great employees that work there and so many great individuals that live there.

It is now 7:00 A.M. The time has come for me to start out on my journey back to work. It has been five months since I was there. I have mixed emotions about facing my fellow employees because my physical appearance is very different than it was the last time they saw me. My face is still very swollen and disfigured by the medication, and I have gone from being 147 pounds to almost 170 pounds. I am wearing dark sunglasses to help dampen the blow. I feel very self-conscious as I travel Interstate 40 West to Conway. The closer I get to Conway, the more anxious I feel. I really have to talk to myself and convince myself that "ALL IS WELL" in spite of how I look. I just can't wait to make it through my first half day of work. I know I will feel better after everyone sees me and then I will be able to adjust and move on. It is now approximately 7:40 A.M. as I pull into the city of Conway. I am about eight minutes away from work. God lets me know that "ALL IS WELL." It is now 7:48 A.M. as I pull into the driveway of my workplace, the Conway Human Development Center. It is dark, it is raining, and it is very stormy. I pull up to the front of the building and I observe many employees standing in the door and looking out of the window awaiting my arrival. This made me feel so wonderful! Several employees ran out of the building to greet me and asked me to give them my car keys so that they could park my car. I was overwhelmed at the love and concern that they showed me. I am beginning to feel a little better since I have already been seen by a few of the employees. The more employees I see the better I will begin to feel. As I enter the building I see a big banner that says, "Welcome back Roy!" As I entered the Staff Development area cheers of welcome back Roy, rang out! I am greeted with hugs and kind words that let me know that they truly missed me and that they are glad that God allowed me a chance to return to work. Many people expressed to me that the word was out that I probably would not survive my illness and that if I survived it, I probably would never be able to return to work. What they had heard was absolutely right but God stepped in and performed a miracle. I am working from 8:00 A.M.-12:00 noon Monday, Wednesday and Friday of this week and next week. I am scheduled to work from 8:00 A.M.-12:00 noon everyday the third week and back to eight hours a day the fourth week. I felt like a kindergarten student when I had to go home at 12 noon each day. I did go straight home to take a nap because for the last five months I have been used to taking several naps a day but "all is well". Employees and individuals who live here have streamed in and out of my office the past few weeks, welcoming me back to work and offering kind words of inspiration. I am adjusting well to being back at work but I am sticking to my dark sunglasses for awhile because my face is very swollen and my eyes are very irritated and very sensitive to light. All of the employees helped me to make the adjustment, although many playfully called me chipmunk cheeks, porky pig, teddy bear and the Pillsbury Dough Boy. We laughed together and had a good time over it. I told them that "ALL IS WELL."

May 24, 1995, was one of the greatest days of my life. It was the day that my wonderful son Eric graduated from J.A. Fair High School in Little Rock. To have my first child to graduate from high school, it was a grand occasion! I had prayed fervently for God to allow me to be well enough to attend the graduation ceremony and He did. I think that if I had not been well enough, I would have told them to bring me anyway, even if they had to bring me on a stretcher. It went so great and I was so proud of my son and to see him graduate. My sister, Laverne Haney, her husband, Dr. Oliver Haney, and their son, Oliver III, made a special trip from Atlanta, Georgia, for the graduation. All of my family from the Little Rock area also attended. I was still very, very weak, but I thank God for allowing me to be alive and to be in attendance. We had a great time! We all took Eric and my nephew Samuel Jordan out to eat at Denny's restaurant where we all congratulated both of them. Samuel had graduated a few days earlier from Parkview High School in Little Rock.

Another great event happened on Sunday, May 28, 1995. I preached an official sermon from the pulpit at the *Williams Temple Church of God In Christ in Little Rock* where I am one of the associate ministers.

I really never stopped preaching during my illness, even when I was lying in the hospital at death's door. This was the first sermon from the pulpit in seven months. I was still very weak, but God blessed in a great way. My subject was "Are You Prepared for the Storm? I encouraged them to be prepared for the storms that are destined to come in their lives, and that if they are not prepared for the storms they won't be able to survive them. I thank God that He allowed me to be prepared for the hurricane that roared through my life. I was prepared because I had already, way before I got deathly ill, constructed a house that was built on

120

a solid rock, and that rock is Jesus. If your house is built on sand, you will not be able to survive the many storms that will come in your life in many, many different ways.

I am reminded of the passage of scripture found in **St. Matthew, Chapter 7 verses 24-27,** Jesus said:

(24) "Therefore whosoever heareth these sayings of mine, and doeth them, I will liken him unto a wise man, which built his house upon a rock":

(25) "And the rain descended, and the floods came, and the winds blew, and beat upon that house; and it fell not: for it was founded upon a rock".

(26) "And every one that heareth these sayings of mine, and doeth them not, shall be likened unto a foolish man, which built his house upon the sand":

(27) "And the rain descended, and the floods came, and the winds blew, and beat upon that house; and it fell: and great was the fall of it".

I want to encourage you to be prepared for the storms that will come in your life and, no matter how difficult the storm, if your house is built on Jesus, you will be able to survive it. I know that there will be many more storms that I will have to face in my life, but I am so thankful to God that I survived this one. The same God that I trusted to bring me through this storm I will also trust for any future ones. I am reminded of a sermon that my brother William preached on one occasion that said "Past Experiences Bring About Present Confidence." This lets me know that the same God that brought me through this storm is able to bring me through the next one, but I must do my part.

Another great example of "Past Experiences Bring About Present Confidence," is when David faced Goliath and slew him. First Samuel Chapter 17 and verses 32-37 says:

(32) And David said to Saul, let no man's heart fail because of him; thy servant will go and fight with this Philistine.

(33) And Saul said to David, Thou art not able to go against this Philistine to fight with him: for thou art but a youth, and he a man of war from his youth.

(34) And David said unto Saul, Thy servant kept his father's sheep, and there came a lion, and a bear, and took a lamb out of the flock:

(35) "And I went out after him, and smote him, and delivered it out of his mouth: and when he arose against me, I caught him by his beard, and smote him, and slew him".

(36) Thy servant slew both the lion and the bear: and this uncircumcised Philistine shall be as one of them, seeing he hath defied the armies of the living God.

(37) David said moreover, The Lord that delivered me out of the paw of the lion, and out of the paw of the bear, he will deliver me out of the hand of this Philistine. And Samuel said unto David, Go, and the Lord be with thee.

I Samuel 17:45 reads:

(45) Then said David to the Philistine, "Thou comest to me with a sword, and with a spear, and with a shield: but I come to thee in the name of the Lord of hosts, the God of the armies of Israel, whom thou hast defied."

So the next time you have a Goliath or a storm in your life, approach it in the name of the Lord and remember the battle is not yours but it's the Lord's. David was victorious over Goliath not by his own strength but by the strength and power of the Lord. I am being victorious over this devastating illness not by my strength but by the strength and power of the Lord!

We had a great time on today. Many of the nurses and staff that took care of me at St. Vincent Hospital came to hear me preach.

They told me while I was still in the hospital to let them know when I would preach my first sermon after being released from the hospital. It made me feel so good because they used their lunch break to come hear me preach. They were still donned in their nurse's uniforms with stethoscopes around their neck. Immediately after I finished they rushed back to the hospital to continue to give wonderful care to their patients, as they had done for me for the 35 days that I was their patient. I will forever be in debt to them. There is a quote that says, "One can repay the loan of gold, but one is forever in debt to those who are kind."

It is now June 1995. I have been back at work a month now. I am adjusting really well. Many employees are still coming and welcoming me back to work. There are over 1200 employees that work here and over 600 individuals who are physically and/or mentally challenged who live here. It will be awhile before I get to see everyone but those who have not been able to come by have called me. Many of the individuals who live here have also been by to welcome me back. I feel so grateful and thankful to God for allowing me the opportunity to work with the fine people here at the Conway Human Development Center, Conway, Arkansas.

My strength is gradually returning. I am able to teach my classes again. I am a Staff Development Specialist in the Staff Training department. We provide training and orientation for new employees and periodic training in various areas for employees who are already here. My job also includes providing supervisory and management training to our supervisory and management staff. I also give tours of our facility for those who are interested.

My classes have been going great. I have to sit down and teach them, which is not my preference, but I am just glad to be back. I am normally more effective in standing up and teaching my classes, but God will provide a way for me to do that in due time. I am still wearing my dark sunglasses even when I teach my classes. While teaching my classes I periodically pick out an employee and tell them that they are not paying attention to what I am saying and that they are not making eye contact with me. They smile and respond by saying "We can't see your eyes!" We always have a lot of fun!

The month of June was also spent teaching my 17 year-old son, Eric, how to drive. I had planned to do that before I got sick so it had to be delayed for awhile. He is making great progress. I am teaching him to drive both an automatic and a standard. We have made many trips over the back roads of the Little Rock area. I am very proud of the great progress that he is making on both vehicles. He has taken his written test and passed.

July, 1995 has arrived and he has found him a job that requires him to have a driver's license. He has passed his written test and they are giving him about a week to take the driving test and produce his driver's license. God blessed us wonderfully. He took his driver's test and passed and was able to keep his job. We are so proud of him. This is his first job after graduating from high school in May of this year. His plans are to enroll in Pulaski Technical College in the fall and work part time.

On Sunday, July 16, 1995, I preached a homecoming service at my brother William's church, the *East End Church of God In Christ,* in Pine Bluff, Arkansas. I am still very weak but God gave me the strength to make it. This is my first visit outside of the city to preach since I became ill. The interesting and exciting thing about this invitation to preach is that it was confirmed while I was still very critically ill. I told my brother to go ahead and schedule me for July 16th because I felt very strongly that God would have me ready by then. So, the date was confirmed by faith and all was well. I was blessed to have in attendance with me, my wife, Marie, my children, Eric and Eboni, and two of my sisters, Queen Esther Ganaway from Little Rock and my sister Mary Johnson from Los Angeles, California. My brother Clinton Johnson from Little Rock and his wife Sharon also attended. We had a great time and God really blessed and confirmed his decision for allowing me to be the guest speaker. God is really blessing me and He is giving me a speedy recovery, considering what I have been through over the last few months. I am deeply grateful to Him for all He has done. July brought about other speaking engagements. I have to keep a light schedule until I get stronger. The spirit is willing but the flesh is weak.

Everyone looks out for me and cautions me not to try to get too much going too soon. I promised that I would be good. My general health is improving daily. My doctor visits are going great and I am able to function a lot better at work. My medication is being decreased, so that means the swelling in my face is going down. I am beginning to look more like myself and fewer people are calling me chipmunk cheeks and Pillsbury Dough Boy. We all had a lot of fun with that.

It is now November 1995 and at my recent visit with Dr. Christopher Adams he and I made the decision to take me completely off of the medication that was causing the swelling and the increase in body weight. I praise God for that. December 1995 is here and I am almost back to normal. I am steadily making significant improvement. My preaching schedule is increasing. During the week of Christmas, I was asked to conduct revival services at the Greater Trinity Church of God In Christ in Little Rock, where the Elder Dewitt Hill is pastor. His church had been faithfully praying for me during my illness, and one of the mothers of the church, Mother Gordy Abraham, would call me at home every Sunday morning to get a report on my progress so that she could inform the church of the miracle that God was working. It was so kind of her to do that and to be so concerned about me. The people at Greater Trinity were so eager to hear my testimony and to see first-hand what God had done through their prayers and of so many other people from around the world. The revival went great and several souls were saved and many people were healed and delivered. This was my first revival since being ill. God really gave me the strength that I needed for the week and He let me know that I was getting back to where I needed to be. I am deeply appreciative to Pastor Dewitt Hill for giving me the great opportunity to spread the Gospel. 1995 ended with a great New Year's Eve watch meeting service at Greater Trinity. Everyone was greatly blessed!

1996 came in while we were rejoicing and praising God in the New Year's Eve service at Greater Trinity.

The great revival service during the week of 1995 at Greater Trinity inspired me to start a worldwide tour in January 1996 to share my testimony. 1994 and 1995 were years of my illness and healing. God spoke to me in January 1996 and told me that it was time to spread the good news to the world about what he had brought me through! I said, "Yes Lord!"

The worldwide tour officially started on Sunday, January 14, 1996 when God led me to go to Elect Temple Church of God In Christ in Benton, Arkansas where the Elder Willie Barnes Jr. is pastor. He gave me an opportunity to preach and to share my testimony. Many were blessed and saved during the service.

The next Sunday, January 21, 1996, God led me to Holy Benton Temple Church of God In Christ in Stuttgart, Arkansas, where the Elder Lawrence O'Neal is the pastor. He gave me the opportunity to preach and to share my testimony. Going to Stuttgart was an extra special trip for me because this is the place where I was born and where I lived for the first 13 years of my life. Also, the Benton Temple Church was the church where I worshiped for the first 13 years of my life under the pastorage of my uncle, the late Elder C.L. Benton. So, this was an opportunity to go back home and share my testimony with many who were there when I was born and with many who had prayed fervently for me during my illness. God really poured out his spirit and again many were saved and many were healed and delivered.

February 1996 led me back to Elect Temple Church of God In Christ in Benton, Arkansas, where Elder Willie Barnes, Jr. is pastor, for a weeklong revival service. The Lord saved and blessed again!

On Sunday, February 11, 1996, God blessed me to preach and share my testimony at St. Paul A.M.E. Church in Morrilton, Arkansas, where Reverend Justus Ready is the pastor. God truly blessed and He has been blessing everywhere that He has been leading me. Where He leads me I will follow.

Reverend Ready is an employee in the Food Services department at St. Vincent Hospital, where I spent 35 days. A co-worker and good friend of mine, Lorraine Brown, told him that she had a friend in the hospital and she asked him if he would go by to see me. He came by shortly after I had been admitted.

He saw me in my weakened and deteriorated condition when I first entered the hospital. He was aware of the revival services that God allowed me to conduct in my room at midnight each night, even when many thought that I would not make it. He saw the miracle that God worked right before the eyes of many. He was so faithful to check on me to see if I needed anything from Food Services. He told me that if what I wanted was not on the menu, just let him know and he would get it for me. I am deeply grateful to Reverend Justice Ready for his kindness. I also express my appreciation to Theresa Parks and Stella Lowe in Food Services for the fine job that they did in caring for me, and I appreciate the entire Food Services staff. All of them did a great job!

My utmost appreciation also goes out to Mrs. Ollie Hall in the housekeeping department for the fine job that she did in taking care of my room and for taking care of the many flowers and plants that friends and family had sent me. James Hall, Alma Jefferson and the entire housekeeping staff deserve high praises for doing such a great job in taking care of my room.

God allowed me many more opportunities in 1996 to share my testimony in revival services that He allowed me to conduct around the state. Some of those places were New Bethel Church of God In Christ, England Arkansas, where Elder Darrell Sanders is pastor; Toones Chapel United Methodist Church, Tulip, Arkansas, where Reverend Roy Smith is the pastor, and Lewis Temple Church of God In Christ, DeQueen, Arkansas, where Elder E.A. Edwards is the pastor.

In 1996 God allowed me to preach and to share my testimony to many other churches, groups and individuals within the state of Arkansas and outside of the state. I was able to share my testimony in person, in places outside of the state such as Texarkana, Texas; Broken Bow, Oklahoma; Memphis, Nashville and Chattanooga, Tennessee; and Atlanta, Georgia. God also blessed me in 1996 to send sermons containing my testimony to places such as Dallas, Texas; Detroit, Michigan; Jersey City, New Jersey; Buffalo, New York; Los Angeles, California; Jackson, Mississippi; Florida, Oklahoma, Georgia and many other places throughout the country. God has truly blessed my tape ministry. Over the past 15 years, He has blessed me to send over 9,000 free copies of sermons all over the United States and to many other parts of the world. He has also blessed me to send out over 10,000 religious tracks and over 50,000 copies of the article that St. Vincent wrote about me while I was in the hospital. These have been distributed all over the United States and throughout the world. God has truly blessed me!

I sincerely thank God for the opportunities that He has allowed me to have to minister to others. As I have attempted to minister to others I have been ministered to by them, because no one can sincerely try to help another without being helped. God has smiled upon me all the days of my life in the good times and the bad times. He promised never to leave me nor to forsake me. "ALL IS WELL."

I am deeply grateful to God for allowing me to experience and to become victorious over my illness. I told someone that if I had known that there would be such a great blessing in being sick, I would have volunteered for it and God would not have had to draft me. The Bible is right! **Romans 8:28** says:

"And we know that all things work together for good to them that love God, to them who are the called according to His purpose."

I meet all of the qualifications of this scripture and everything that I have suffered has certainly worked together for the good. I thank Him for counting me worthy enough to suffer for Him, considering all of the things that He suffered for me.

1996 ended on a great note with me being in revival services in DeQueen, Arkansas. I was up preaching the gospel and sharing my testimony when 1997 came in.

I look forward to God doing greater things for me in 1997.

My worldwide tour for 1997 was launched at the First Baptist Church, 9th and Calhoun Streets, here in Little Rock. This is where the Reverend Antonio Scruggs is the interim pastor. I was there on the 2nd and 3rd Sundays in January 1997. Again, God richly blessed, as I was able to preach and share my testimony of the great things that God has done for me. Many were blessed and one came to Christ.

Jesus says in **St. Luke 15:7,**

"I say unto you, that likewise joy shall be in heaven over one sinner that repenteth, more than over ninety and nine just persons, which need no repentance."

I received a call the other day from Elder Willie Barnes, Jr., pastor of Elect Temple Church of God In Christ in Benton, Arkansas. He asked me to come back in February of this year and do another week of revival services. I also did a week revival at his church in February 1996. 1997 has already shown signs of being another great year of traveling and preaching and sharing my testimony about the goodness of the Lord with the world. It is up to each one of us to work and do what we can for the Lord while we have a chance. Jesus said in **St. John 9:4,**

"I must work the works of him that sent me, while it is day; the night cometh, when no man can work."

Sometimes we have great things that we like do for the Lord and simply because we may not always be able to accomplish the so-called great things, sometimes we choose to do nothing but the smallest deed is worth more than the greatest intention. So, it is very important to do what you can regardless of how large or small it may appear to be. I am reminded of a little story that I heard about the little sparrow and a mighty horse. One day the mighty horse came down the road and saw a little tiny sparrow lying flat of his back in the middle of the road with his legs in the air. The mighty horse looked at the little sparrow and became puzzled at what he saw. He said, "Why are you lying in the middle of the road looking so stupid with your skinny little legs in the air?"

The little sparrow responded that he heard that the sky was falling and he was just trying to hold it up.

The mighty horse said, "You must be crazy. You can't hold anything up with your skinny little legs, and you should get out of the middle of the road looking so stupid."

The little sparrow responded for the last time and said, "one does what one can!"

With God what we consider to be our little turns into much. God is always able to multiply whatever we do for Him. It is our responsibility to trust Him with all of our heart, even in the midst of dark and difficult situations. Faith and doubt cannot stay in the same room together, but faith and its first cousin trust can. Faith sustains us in confusing times. Faith and trust in God that He has everything under control supports us when the way seems unclear. We can believe that things will ultimately work out.

There is a story about a group of botanists who were searching for a rare flower. After weeks of searching, they found it. There was a problem. The flower was at the bottom of a steep cliff. The only way down was to be lowered by rope. All the botanists were a little more than pleasingly plump. As they were discussing their plight, a small boy walked up. "What are you doing?" he asked.

"Aha!" they thought, "Here is the answer to our problem. Young man, will you let us tie this rope to you and lower you down to get that flower? We'll pay you ten dollars." "I don't know," he replied, and he took off running. "Twenty dollars!" the botanist shouted. "Forty!"

The boy kept running. In just a minute he was back, pulling a man with him by the hand.

"So you've reconsidered our offer?" they asked hopefully. "Shucks, mister I'll do it for nothing." The boy replied, "I just wanted my dad to hold the rope."

We can do anything, as long as we know that God is holding the rope!

CHILDHOOD, TEENAGE YEARS AND MANHOOD IN STUTTGART, ARKANSAS AND LITTLE ROCK, ARKANSAS

Living and growing up in Stuttgart, which is the Rice and Duck capital of the world, was a great opportunity as well as a great experience. Many things that I learned and that I was taught in Stuttgart as a child helped set the stage for me to effectively handle and deal with things that I would face as a teenager and as an adult. My childhood in Stuttgart was a very rewarding one. God blessed me to be born to two of the greatest parents in the world: William and Laura Johnson! To compliment my wonderful parents, He also blessed me with many wonderful brothers and sisters. There were fifteen of us children in the family. I was the baby, or the youngest child for about two years, from 1950-1952. In 1952, God blessed my parents with a beautiful little baby daughter whose name was Brenda Louise Johnson. I was about two years old at this time and my speech was still in its developing stage, so I very affectionately called her, "Breeze", trying to say Brenda Louise. The unfortunate thing is that Brenda was born with many medical problems and had many surgeries and many complications from the surgeries.

She passed away within a couple of years after she was born. I very vividly remember seeing this beautiful little baby lying on the bed and being attended to by other members of the family. I remember the smiles that she gave, the cries that she made and the joy that she brought to all of us. We were all deeply saddened when she left us. Even though I didn't quite understand everything at the moment, I realized that there was great joy in the home for awhile and a beautiful little baby and it seemed that almost as quickly as the joy came, it also left. Sadness engulfed the home and once again I became the main focus of attention in the family. Even now, moments of sadness overshadow me as I reflect upon the blessings that I may have missed by not having the opportunity to grow up with her.

Brenda Louise Johnson will forever have a special place in my heart. I am thankful to God that at least for a brief period of time, I got to be one of her big brothers that she had to care for her and for her to look up to.

In 1955, when I was about five years old, my family and I had eaten fish for supper. I vividly recall realizing that there was an uncomfortable feeling in my throat. The uncomfortable feeling intensified. I became very alarmed and began to cry and my parents concluded that I had gotten a fish bone in my throat. They began to tell me several things to do to get the bone out but nothing worked. I became more afraid because the pain was getting worse and the bone was not moving and every time I swallowed I felt it. I then called very loudly for "Sister Julia." Sister Julia was an older lady who lived next door, Sister Julia Pendelton. I would always see her with her fishing poles in her car and she would be on her way somewhere to fish. I felt that if anyone could help get the bone out of my throat she could. Sister Julia was summoned and she helped my parents get the bone out. I was so relieved and it was a very long time before I wanted to eat fish again.

I was to be the focus of attention and the center of attraction for the Johnson family for about two years after my little sister's sudden departure. On January 11, 1956, another little baby was born into the Johnson family. This time it was a little baby boy by the name of Clinton Earl Johnson. Again, much joy filled the Johnson home over the fact that God allowed another baby to be added to the Johnson family. Clint, as we call him, became my wonderful little brother.

In 1958, when I was around eight years old, I was returning home from the store when I was greeted by a little fierce, barking daschund or wiener dog. I became frightened as I observed the little dog in his yard and not tied up. I immediately decided that I probably needed to speed things up a little bit before he came out to get me. As I sped things up, the little dog chased me. I ran and ran until I ran out of breath and stumbled and fell. When this happened he caught up with me and bit me on the back of the neck and he ran back to his yard. God blessed that the bite was not serious and required no medical attention.

As I lay in the street screaming, I realized that I made the wrong decision to run. I learned a great lesson. Anytime thereafter that I had to pass that way, I made sure that I had a pocket full of rocks just in case the little dog tried to bite me again.

This incident occurred close to the home of some older people who always sat on the porch during favorable weather. We called them Uncle Charlie and Mama Lucy. Each time we would pass their house, we would greet them and offer to bring in some water or wood for them, or to see if they needed anything from the store. They were between 80 and 90 years old. I would often just stop by and listen to their words of wisdom. They always had some good advice to give us children and something very interesting, exciting and profitable to say. They taught me a lot about life. Their last name was Pendleton.

Another family in Stuttgart that inspired me was the Offords. Sister Essie Mae and Brother John as we called them. They would always treat us so kindly and were always excited and glad to see us. I remember on one occasion Sister Essie cooked a cake but forgot to put sugar in it. One of my brothers said, "Sister Essie Mae, this cake don't have any sugar in it." We still remind her to make sure that she doesn't forget the sugar! As we grew up in Stuttgart, not only were we blessed to have wonderful parents, but we were also blessed to have a wonderful uncle and aunt, Elder C.L. Benton and his wife, Mrs. Alberta Benton, my mother's sister. Both are now deceased. Uncle Benton, as we called him was like a second dad to us. My dad worked out of town and came home on the weekends. Uncle Benton took us under his wings and allowed us to go practically everywhere he went. He was pastor of Benton Temple Church of God In Christ in Stuttgart, Arkansas, which is the church that we grew up in. Our neighbors also helped to raise us and were a part of our family. To name a few, Bro. Bob Pendelton and his wife Sister Julia, Mr. Loggie Blake and his wife, Mrs. Byce, Ms. Barbara Allen,

Ms. Zola and Mr. Tot, Bro. Willie Pendleton and his wife, Sis. Helen, and Bro. Reece Pendelton and his wife Sister Esther, Mr. Henry Hubbard, Mr. Hill and his wife Ms. Sadie, Rev. Robert Vanderbilt and his wife Mrs. Jewel, and Mrs. Collier. Mr. Andrew Tolbert taught us how to plow with his mules and would often allow us to ride in his mule driven wagon to the Kroger store in downtown Stuttgart. I had a very wonderful and interesting childhood with so many people who cared about me and who would teach me the right thing. One of my favorite things to do as a child was to visit the older people and listen to their words of wisdom. One man in particular was Mr. Henry Hubbard and his son, Theodore. Theodore was physically disabled and lived with his dad on Rose Street, about a block from my house. Mr. Henry Hubbard was about 75 years old when I was a little boy, and Theodore was about 55 years old. Theodore did not have a wheelchair but he sat in and used a cain bottom chair to get around through the house. Mr. Hubbard had a 1938 model Ford car and 1949 Ford truck. Both were a joy to be around. Theodore passed the time by being an expert in the game of washers. Most of the children in the neighborhood would gather at the Hubbard's to compete in a game of washers with the king of the game of washers, Mr. Theodore Hubbard. We very seldom won against Theodore. Theodore was also an expert marksman with a BB gun. These two gentlemen taught me a lot about life and how to be respectful to your parents, other adults and everyone else. I will never forget the impact that they had on my life. My parents, William and Laura Johnson, and my many brothers and sisters also had a great positive effect on my life. I had some great role models. My brothers and sisters include: William Johnson, Preston Johnson, Freddie Ray Johnson, Queen Esther Ganaway, Edna Clayborn, Mary Johnson, Samuel Johnson, Laverne Haney, Charles Johnson, James Johnson, Clinton Johnson. My sister Brenda and my brothers DeArthur and Theoplis Johnson are now deceased. My brothers and sisters always looked out for me. I worked all my life around the house and sometimes I would get upset with my sister Laverne because there were many days when I would be out playing and having the time of my life and she would come to the back door of our house and call my name at the top of her voice. When I was growing up everyone called me "Roy Henry". Wherever I may have been, I was always in hearing distance. Sometimes I responded and sometimes I did not because I knew that she had swept the house and left the trash in a pile and wanted me to come and pick it up. I always wondered why she couldn't just go ahead and finish the job. I found out later that she was just teaching me the value of work. We laugh about that even now.

My first job away from home was in 1959 at the age of nine. At this time I was hired by my next door neighbor Bro. Bob Pendelton to feed and take care of his chickens. He was physically disabled and was very limited in what he could do. He paid me $0.35 a week. I would feed, water and gather the eggs for him. I would also have to go in the chicken house to retrieve them when they died. This was a great opportunity for me and taught me responsibility at an early age. Bro. Bob and his wife, Sister Julia were always so nice to us. We never had a television while in Stuttgart, so they would let us visit their house on Saturday night to watch television with them. Bro. Bob would always buy a big bag of chocolate covered peanut M&M's and he would always pour some out of the bag into his hands and offer them to us and he would imitate the famous M&M commercial and say, "Melts in your mouth, not in your hands."

As a young child I was very, very stingy. I was probably one of the stingiest kids in the neighborhood. A classic example of this is one day when Bro. Bob paid me the $0.35 that I had earned for a week's work, I went to the local grocery store, which was owned by Mrs. Eva Mae Keeble and bought me a big sack of cookies that I had planned to eat all by myself. I knew that if I went home and went in the house that my brothers and sister would want some of them. This particular day I decided that I would avoid all family and friends by entering a place of seclusion so that I could eat all my cookies in peace and without having to have anyone around to beg for them or to take them away from me. I got this bright idea that rather than going in the house that I would be better off to go under the house. I nearly choked to death on the cookies. I started gagging very loudly and it was heard by those who were inside the house. They knew we didn't have a dog so my brother Charles ran and looked under the house and crawled under there and pulled me out and helped to save my life. He found out that the noise was being made by his stingy little brother Roy. I have always been deeply grateful to him for helping to save my life. I am now very freehearted. If I only had one cookie I would have enough cookies to share with others and I would still have enough cookies for myself. I was about nine years old when this incident happened. God was not ready for me yet! Praise God!

Another incident that happened when I was about nine years old also could have been fatal. I was playing a game of running around the house with some friends. We would run around the house several times. As I was making a turn around the back of the house by the water hydrant, my foot slipped in a wet area by the hydrant and the corner of my left hand fell in the middle of some very large pieces of glass from a broken bottle that had been left around the hydrant. As I lay there bleeding profusely, my mother was summoned to the rear of the house and heard my screams and observed blood gushing from my hand. She immediately contacted a neighbor who had a vehicle and I was rushed to the doctor's office. The doctor performed surgery on my hand and removed several large pieces of broken glass from my hand and sewed it up.

About nine months after the incident occurred, my hand still had not completely healed. My parents became concerned, and I was taken back to the doctor, surgery was performed again and another large piece of glass was removed from my hand that had been lodged there for the past nine months. This certainly could have been fatal or could have set some kind of poisoning that could have caused my hand or arm to be amputated. God was certainly looking out for me again, as He has done all my life. I am so grateful to Him for sparing my life and my hand and arm.

My mother, sister, and brothers took good care of me and my little brother while dad was out of town working during the week. When my brothers and I were bad during the week, my mother and my sister would report us to dad and we would get a whipping when he arrived home on Saturday. Sometimes we would get one whether we did anything or not. Dad would say, "if you didn't do anything this time you will probably do something before I get back this weekend!" This would be for the old and the new. Oftentimes when my mother and sister would see and hear us getting a whipping they would regret that they told on us.

Mom and dad worked hard to help keep things going for us. Mom worked in various cafeterias in Stuttgart while we were growing up. Places like City Café and Max's Café in Stuttgart, Arkansas.

This was during segregation when there were white and colored sections of the cafeteria and white and colored entrances. Even though my mother worked at these cafeterias, whenever we would go there, she, as well as the rest of us would have to enter through the colored entrance and eat in the colored section. This was also the case at the Greyhound Bus Station. There were white and colored entrances, white and colored sections, white and colored bathrooms and white and colored water fountains. I learned a lot about life and a lot about people during these times. Dad also worked hard, oftentimes working two jobs during the week in Little Rock. Mom would work hard all day and go to church at night. We grew up at Benton Temple Church of God In Christ in Stuttgart, where the late Elder C.L. Benton was pastor. My mother would call from work and have me and my little brother Clint to get ready and meet her at church. The church was about five blocks from our house, so we would walk to church and be there when she got there between 8:00 P.M. and 8:30 P.M. each night.

When my dad would prepare to go back to Little Rock on Sunday evening, I would ask him if I could walk him part of the way to the bus station to help him carry his suitcase. He would always say yes. These were great moments for me to spend time all by myself with my dad, walking and talking and asking him lots of questions. He very seldom made it to the bus station because he had become a professional at hitchhiking rides with people. Practically everyone knew him and would always be glad to give him a ride as far as they were going and he would eventually make it to Little Rock. I would often have tears in my eyes because dad was gone for another week. I would very sadly return back home to wait for dad to return the next week. I would always take great consolation in knowing that dad would not forget about me, even though he was away. I would always with great anticipation, look for a letter from dad every Wednesday of the week that he was gone and by the way, he would always include a dime in the letter, just for me. He always remembered. The letter was delivered by our postman, Mr. Brown, who first walked all over the neighborhood delivering mail, and then later by bicycle. I was between the ages of five and 11 years old. The letter would be addressed to Master Roy Henry Johnson. This would be sprawled in big letters across the envelope in my dad's very unique style of writing. This made me so happy to know that my dad cared enough to keep in touch with me. It made me feel very special! But as time went on and my little brother Clint was born in 1956 and as he grew up, dad would still send the dime but I would have to give a nickel of it to my little brother. I was hurt but it taught me how to share with others. Times were tough and wages were low and dad could not afford to send two dimes so I had to adjust but "ALL IS WELL!" As I recount these experiences I am thankful and grateful to God for the wonderful childhood experiences that He allowed me to have and the wonderful family that He allowed me to be born into. We didn't have many material possessions but we were rich in love and in the things that be of the spirit of God, which I know are far greater possessions than the material ones. The material things perish but the spiritual things linger. The material things that I had as a child are gone but the things that I learned about God and His son Jesus are still in my heart. I will forever cherish the experiences that I had growing up in a home with my dad, my mother, my sisters, brothers and all other family members, church members, neighbors, friends, schoolmates, teachers and everyone else who has inspired me along life's way.

Another great experience during my childhood was the trips that we made to our summer home in Woodson, Arkansas. Dad worked in Little Rock during the week but lived in Woodson, which is about 20 miles south of Little Rock, and came to Stuttgart to be with the family on the weekend. Stuttgart is about 50 miles east of Little Rock. So you can see that it was a lot easier to hitchhike a ride to Woodson every day rather than hitchhiking a ride to Stuttgart, since we didn't have a car. It was in Woodson during the summer that we learned the art of working hard, tilling the ground and staying out of trouble. It was a great experience being in a very rural setting at this time. During the fifties this was considered going to the country. We had an opportunity to chop wood, tend to the chickens, go to the well to draw water, take care of the garden, plow the fields, and pick or chop cotton. I was one of the younger ones, so a whole lot was not required of me and my little brother Clint but my brothers James and Charles, who are twins, and my brother DeArthur Johnson, who is now deceased, had greater opportunities than I did to chop cotton and till the ground. My brother Charles would often find a way to miss the cotton chopping bus during the early hours of the morning. He became very skilled at coming up with an acceptable explanation to dad as to the reason why he missed the bus. We would often go back to Stuttgart to be with the rest of the family on the weekend. Many of our friends really didn't know where we were going during the summer. Many thought that we were vacationing in some faraway place and many times we never corrected their train of thought.

Another incident that I very vividly remember occurred with my deceased brother DeArthur. This happened around 1961.

I was 11 years old and he was 17. He was left in charge and I was to obey him. It all started when I disobeyed a command that he had given me. Before this incident I had an excellent record of doing what he asked me to do and I had shown a lot of respect to him. For some reason, on this particular day in the spring of 1961, I decided that I didn't want to do what he had asked me to do. He was in a total state of shock upon hearing my response. I don't think that he thought he heard me correctly, so he gave me an opportunity to change my mind. Again I told him that I was not going to do what he asked me to do. Of course, I had to suffer the consequences of disobedience but not before engaging in a foot race with him all over the neighborhood and down the railroad tracks. I soon realized that I was no match for him. I began to get weak and tired and finally ran out of breath. He caught me and whipped me back to the house and I decided that it was best for everyone, including me, that I repent and do what I was asked to do. He told me after both of us had gotten to be adults that he really admired me for standing up to him and for standing up for what I believed that I should or should not do, even though I was wrong. He said that this was the beginning of me becoming a man. Up until about three days before his death, on January 8, 1994, we laughed and talked about the incident that had occurred 33 years earlier, although he still told me that I was very wrong for disobeying him.

There were many other people who inspired me as a child while growing up in Stuttgart. Among them was the Holmes family: Elder A.B. Holmes, who built the house that we lived in and his wife, Mother Holmes and their children Ora Lee and Mae Willie.

Mother Holmes was in charge of the Vacation Bible School and made it very interesting and exciting for the children. I remember pushing my little brother Clint down the road in his stroller to the Vacation Bible School. Elder Holmes gave me a little plum tree that I took home and planted and it grew and produced some very delicious plums. So delicious that around the age of ten, I became a fence builder. I constructed a fence around my plum tree to try to keep the other little kids from getting all of my plums. Needless to say, it did not work. Somehow while I would be away from home, I would come back and notice that the fence had been tampered with and more of my plums were gone.

During this time I also had a pet rooster that I took care of and I used to cook for him. I would go out back of the house in my mother's green patch and pick some greens for my rooster and then in the middle of garden I gathered some bricks and constructed a little fireplace that I used to cook the greens on. I would get one of my mother's pots and also a pan and some meal so that I could cook him some cornbread to go along with his greens. The rooster loved me and I loved him. One day the food got low and the rooster had to die. It was very difficult to watch as his neck was twisted from his body and he became dinner for the family. I was very saddened and depressed for a long period of time. I did ask for and received his neck. I dug a little grave and buried it under my plum tree. I also constructed a small cross to mark the grave with. This was the kind that I had seen them make on Gunsmoke. I was around ten years old at this time.

Another interesting and exciting thing for me as a child was getting a chance to stop by the Mulberry tree. This was always a great treat. There were several of them in the neighborhood and it was a great gathering ground for many of the children while out playing.

There were many grocery stores that we would frequent in the neighborhood. One of them was Ms. Eva Mae Keebles store. We would often help her put up groceries. She would pay us in cookies and candy, which satisfied us well. We were great friends of her son, Donald Keeble. Another store was Mr. Solomon's. He was a very intelligent and astute older gentleman who always instructed us with sound words of wisdom. I would often be sent to his store by my mother to buy $0.25 worth of sugar. He would keep the sugar in a big barrel and dip it out into a small brown bag and weigh it on the scales. This was a very happy time of my life.

The next store was Ms. Hicks grocery store. She was a white lady who was always so nice and kind to our family. We would often go to her store and she would allow us to charge things on our family bill at the store. My mother and dad would pay on the bill at the store until it was paid out. It would have been very difficult for us to make it through the tough times that we faced growing up if it had not been for the kindness of the storekeepers in our community such as Mr. Solomon Johnson, Ms. Eva Mae Kebble and Ms. Hicks, who all allowed us to make charges at their stores way before VISA, American Express and MasterCard were discovered. Another store that we would frequent was owned by the white people. When asked where we were going, we would say that we were going to the "white store".

This is how it was distinguished from the other stores. They were also very nice to us. They had a son who was in college who later became a state representative.

I was born in 1950 and a good friend of mine, L.C. Hill was also born around 1950. There were several children in our family and we didn't always have the finances to get everything that we needed. Finances were very low at the time that I was born and my family could not afford to buy me a milk bottle but they were able to get a nipple for a bottle. L.C. was fortunate enough to have both. This is humorous but it is very true. My parents would borrow the bottle from L.C. when he was not using it so that I could use it. When I finished drinking milk out of it, it would be sterilized and returned to L.C. As we got older we had a lot of fun talking about our sharing of the same milk bottle.

Later in life things got better for us. My dad was able to buy a bright red 1954 International truck that all of us were ashamed to ride in. The other children often teased us for having a red fire truck. My dad was very proud of his truck and our family would load up and go on our merry way in the "little red fire truck".

There was a man in the neighborhood that owned a mule team. His name was Mr. Andrew Tolbert. He often would hire me out to help him plow the fields and haul things for people on his wagon. Even though I got to work for Mr. Tolbert some, his right hand man was a good friend of mine by the name of Franklin Vanderbilt. Mr. Tolbert would often take us children on a wagon ride through downtown Stuttgart in the 50's and early 60's to the Kroger store at the south end of Buerkle Street. We had the time of our lives. Sometimes he would even allow us to assist him in driving the mule team.

During my early childhood in Stuttgart, I attended elementary school during the first grade at Holman High School. This school served grades 1-12. My first grade teacher's name was Ms. Baxter. My second and third grade years were spent at a new three-room red schoolhouse that was closer to my home. My second grade teacher was Ms. Briggs and my third grade teacher was Ms. Phillips. We often went to Metcalf store after school. My 4th, 5th and 6th grade years were spent at Park Avenue Elementary School in Stuttgart. My 4th grade teacher's name was Ms. Nellie Jean Noble, 5th grade, Ms. Helen Cyrus, and my 6th grade teacher was Mr. Moss. During my 6th grade year I became a member of the school safety patrol. I started as a Private but worked my way up to Sergeant before the school year was over. It was a very interesting and challenging job. The other children kind of looked up to me. I was real proud to be a member of the school safety patrol. Knowing that by standing near the school with my long pole with a red flag on it stopping traffic so the other children could cross the street safely was a very rewarding experience, especially for a 12-year old. Each day other children from the neighborhood and I would run home for lunch and return in 30 minutes for our afternoon classes. Our house was about five blocks from Park Avenue School.

For my seventh grade year I returned back across town to Holman High School, which had grades 1-12. There was not a black junior high school in my neighborhood. Things were still very segregated in Stuttgart and many other places around the country during this time. The black students would receive the discarded books of the students at the white school, whenever they got new ones. It was tough, but by the help of God, we made it. I would often walk to town to the post office and to businesses to pay bills for my parents. I would often be subjected to racial insults on the way. Most of the time I was able to turn my head and ignore them. God made us all and I couldn't understand then nor can I understand now why there is such a big fuss over the color of one's skin. It takes all colors to make up a rainbow and I've never seen a piano that didn't have both black and white keys on it. It is ridiculous and it is utterly non-sense for us to involve ourselves in such trivial matters. Let's build bridges, not walls!

At Holman I was reunited with friends that I had known since first grade. My tenure at Holman was very short-lived, only two months. My youngest brother, Clint, had been plagued with recurring bouts with asthma. It became very life threatening. The doctor advised us that we had to move to a different environment because if he had another major attack, he probably would not survive it. The dust and other allergic pathogens in the Stuttgart area proved to be too much for him. We immediately loaded up my dads "little red fire truck", as we called it, and moved to Little Rock. After moving to Little Rock, Clint had no problems with his asthma. It was difficult losing friends that I had known practically all of my life, but it would have been more difficult to lose a brother that I had known all of his life.

November 1963 we moved to Little Rock, where I enrolled as a 7th grade student at Booker Jr. High School. I was 13 years old.

It didn't take long for me to make new friends. One of the first friends that I made in 1963 was a young man by the name of James Yarbough, and we are still great friends in 1997. We moved to the Booker Homes housing project in the Granite Mountain area of Little Rock. Our address was 26 Burbank Drive. All of my friends from Stuttgart thought that I had moved to a mansion based on my new address, but, of course, I had not. The address just sounded that way. Being in the city and living in the project provided many temptations for a 13-year-old just moving from a rural area. I saw many things that I had never seen before and was in an environment like I had never been in before. I am thankful to God that I was raised in a Christian home with Christian parents who didn't just send us to church, but went with us to church. I am also thankful to God that I had older brothers and sisters who were great role models for me. All of them always instructed me in the right way. So even though I was in a different environment, I didn't allow the different environment to overshadow the things that I had been taught. I was not perfect but I did not allow myself to be persuaded to attach myself with the wrong crowd. Dad worked two jobs during this time and mom did private home work.

After completing Booker Jr. High in May of 1965, I enrolled in Horace Mann High School in Little Rock as a sophomore in the fall of 1965. My brothers James and Charles Johnson who are twins had just graduated from Horace Mann in May of 1965 and had made a great name for themselves and everyone: including the Principal Mr. Edwin Hawkin, the vice Principal Mr. Willie Thompson and the teachers and students were happy to know that I was James and Charles Johnson's little brother. All of this made it easier for me in some ways and then more difficult in other ways. They had made such a great name for themselves, and everyone had the same high expectations for me. I knew the great challenge that I had ahead of me and I don't think that I disappointed anybody. My brother Charles was president of his senior class, which impressed me greatly. My sophomore year at Horace Mann was spent getting to know everybody at the school, including the teachers, students and the school staff. There were about 900 students at Horace Mann during this time. I met a lot of people and made a lot of friends during my first year there. In my junior year, which began in the fall of 1966, I developed some political ambitions. I had been reflecting on the good record that my twin brothers had made there and I decided that I would try to walk in their footsteps. With the encouragement of my brothers and other family members and friends that I had made at school, I decided that I would run for the office of president of my junior class. I won my first election with an overwhelming majority of the votes. This encouraged me and gave me a lot of confidence for my future ambitions. We had a great year! Also during my junior year I became a member of the DECA program, which stands for Distributive Education Clubs of America. This was a program in which students were taught and encouraged to become future leaders in the business world. The students would go to school for half a day and then be placed in a local business to work in the afternoon. I really enjoyed this program. The advisor, who was a fine gentleman, was the late Mr. R.J. Altheimer. I was greatly inspired by him. My brother James had been a part of the program and recommended that I join. It was a great decision that I made. In the spring of 1967 we were preparing for our state DECA conference which was held at the Marion Hotel in Little Rock. Mr. Altheimer approached me to see if I was interested in running for a state office during this conference. I told him that I would think about it and would let him know. A few days later I talked with him and told him that I was interested in running for state vice-president of DECA. He was concerned about my decision to run for vice–president since most of the schools in Arkansas were still segregated and that I would be the first black person to run for that office and my competition would be white and the great majority of the students at the conference would be white. He stated that the secretary, or treasurer, or sergeant-at-arms would be a more realistic goal but he told me that he would support me in whatever decision that I made. After advising me of the competition that I would be facing he asked me again what was my decision. I graciously thanked him for the information, but my decision was still to run for state vice-president of DECA. He applauded me for my determination and said that he would do everything that he could to help me. I also had the support of the students from Horace Mann who were a part of DECA. Mr. Altheimer immediately set out to help me. He first consulted with the school's print shop and had campaign cards printed up. About 400 people were in attendance at the convention. I had more than enough cards for everyone who attended. I began to plan my strategy and began to develop campaign speeches for the conference. My fellow students in the DECA program at Horace Mann were willing to be my campaign workers. The conference was held in March 1967. I personally greeted and shook hands with all who were attending the conference and asked them for their vote. We had opportunities to make speeches before the election. My friends from school passed out campaign cards and also greeted those who were in attendance. On election day I became the first black officer and the first black vice-president of the state

DECA Club. Jim Riley from Hot Springs was elected state president that year. We had a great working relationship. In April 1967 we attended the National DECA Convention at the Conrad Hilton Hotel on Michigan Avenue in Chicago, Illinois. My good friend John Lovelace was the other student from Horace Mann who went to the convention. This was my first time out of state and it was truly an amazing adventure. I had heard so much about the things that go on in Chicago. When we arrived there, I was overwhelmed by the tall buildings, the many people, and the Hilton Hotel that we would be staying in. John and I stayed on the 28th floor. Neither one of us had ever been up that high before. There were major concerns on the part of both of us. Immediately upon entering the room I found the nearest window. Our room faced Lake Michigan. As I looked out of the window and down to the ground a feeling of dizziness engulfed me. I became very weak and had to move speedily away from the window. Later in the week a light snowfall occurred. Again I approached the window and became brave enough to raise it and watch the beautiful snowflakes as they passed my window on the 28th floor and then plummeted down 28 floors to the ground. I had never seen anything so fascinating in my life. We had a great National DECA conference. We were there for a week. As we became involved in the conference activities, one of the delegates from Arkansas who was aware of the successful campaign I had in winning the election for vice-president of the state DECA program approached me about being her campaign manager for her run for a National DECA office.

I gladly accepted the challenge and the campaign was on. I had the opportunity to make speeches on her behalf to thousands of delegates from around the country. We were not successful in winning the election, but we won a chance to grow and to develop. We fought a good fight. It was a wonderful opportunity and a great learning experience.

With the experiences at the National DECA Conference still fresh in my mind, I looked for another challenge during my senior year at Horace Mann.

I had won the presidency of my junior class and thought about seeking the presidency of my senior class as my brother Charles had done and won.

While I pondered over the run for senior class president a greater challenge beckoned for me. I was urged by my fellow students to run for president of the entire student body of 900 students. The student council. I gladly accepted the challenge to run for president of the student council. Again, another campaign was on. I shook a lot of hands and made a lot of speeches. On election day I was declared the winner by a landslide vote. I was thrilled that again my fellow students had put confidence in me, this time to lead the entire student body. We had a great year and it was a great learning experience for me. At the end of the school year I made my farewell address to the students. Upon seeking some material to use for my farewell address to the students, I found a very moving and touching farewell address that my brother Charles had written when he was senior class president.

I must confess that I borrowed heavily from his speech and mixed it in with what I was able to do on my own and it was superb! The students and teachers came up after the assembly and told me how much they were moved by the speech and how they had to fight back the tears as I spoke. God was with me and I am glad that he allowed me the opportunity to have such wonderful experiences and opportunities in high school.

In the fall of 1968, I enrolled as a freshman at Philander Smith College in Little Rock. Again the challenge was on and I could not pass it up. I was encouraged by my fellow freshmen classmates to run for president of my freshman class. Again I gladly accepted the challenge and the campaign for freshman class president was on. This campaign was a little different from the ones in high school. In high school it was limited to students from around the city of Little Rock, many of whom I already knew. At Philander it was students from around the state and the world, most of whom I did not know. I quickly got to know them and on election day I was declared the winner by an overwhelming majority. Needless to say I was urged to run again for president of my sophomore class, my Junior class and, yes, my senior class also. God blessed me to win all of them. I very graciously thanked my fellow students for putting their trust and confidence in me to lead them for the entire 4 years that we were there. Again these were opportunities that allowed me to grow and to develop. Opportunities and experiences that I will cherish for the rest of my life.

In July of 1969 at the age of 19, while visiting my dad in Woodson, Arkansas, I was stung by a bee, while helping him with some chores outside. To my knowledge I had never been stung by a bee before and was not aware of any possible allergic reactions to them. Within a short period of time after being stung I began to feel very weak and fatigued. I became very concerned about what was happening. The temperature that day was probably 95 degrees. I was already hot from being outside and it appeared that my body temperature was rising. I immediately determined that I needed to seek medical attention. I immediately went to the University of Arkansas Medical Center in Little Rock to seek treatment in the emergency room. While waiting to see a doctor, I began to feel abnormal changes in the skin on my face. Whelps and wrinkles began to appear. I became very alarmed and concerned about what was happening to me and the possible consequences of it. I found a mirror and looked in it and I became more alarmed than ever. My whole facial appearance had changed. I had the facial wrinkles of a 95 year old man and I was only 19. Fleeting thoughts as to whether this would be a permanent appearance the rest of my life plagued my consciousness. I was very relieved and comforted after visiting with the doctor as he assured me that there was something that he could do to help me. After receiving an injection and other treatments, I was discharged from the emergency room. Within a short period of time my skin began to return to normal. The whelps and the wrinkles began to slowly disappear. Before long I was totally back to normal. This was a very traumatic experience and one that I will never, ever forget. I thanked God for blessing me that day and for allowing everything to turn out well.

In the fall of 1970, I was introduced to a very beautiful and charming young lady at Philander Smith College by the name of Lillie Marie Page from Rosston, Arkansas. I was introduced to her by her cousin Syble Moss. This was my junior year and this was her freshman year. Needless to say, we became very attached to each other and we were married on July 21, 1973, at 6:00 P.M. at Mt. Moriah United Methodist Church in Chidester, Arkansas, by Rev. Fred Walters. This was my wife's home church at the time. We have been married for 24 years and have two wonderful children: Eric (age 20) and Eboni (age 16).

In May of 1972, I graduated from Philander Smith College in Little Rock with a B.A. degree. I purchased my first automobile with help from my dad who cosigned for me. It was a brand new light–blue Volkswagen. It cost $2,000, and I paid $300 down and $75 a month. I could fill it up with gas to the brim for only $2.98 and could drive a week or more on it. In August of 1972, I enrolled in a master's program in Counseling at the University of Central Arkansas in Conway. Also in August 1972, I was hired as a substitute teacher in the Little Rock school district; I substituted 3 days a week on Monday, Wednesday and Friday. I had classes at UCA during the day on Tuesday and Thursday, and classes at night on Monday and Wednesday. God really blessed me where I could take a full graduate school class load and work also. This was a great opportunity because in one of my night classes, I met the principal of Booker Jr. High School, Mr. Eugene Keaton. He then started requesting me to substitute at his school on a regular basis on Monday, Wednesday and Friday. When I completed my master's degree in Counseling in August 1973, he immediately hired me as a full-time teacher in the special education department at Booker. I taught at Booker from August 1973 to May 1974. Returning to a school to teach where I had been a student 10 years earlier was a wonderful opportunity.

They were extremely proud of me and I was very proud of myself. I got a chance to sit in the teachers lounge. I had always wondered as a student what went on in there. I got a chance to attend faculty meetings with teachers who had taught me. It was a real rewarding experience for me.

At the end of May of 1974 I accepted a staff development specialist job with the State of Arkansas, working with the Department of Human Services, Developmental Disabilities Division at 18th and Maple Street in North Little Rock. The office soon moved to the Waldon Building at 7th and Main Street in Little Rock.

From 1976 to 1977 the agency afforded me the opportunity to improve my training and management skills by allowing me to attend the management training program at the University of Alabama in Birmingham. I completed this program in April of 1977. This was one of the greatest training opportunities that I have ever had. Two persons at the program that had a major positive effect on my life during training were Dr. Bill Garove, the director of the management training program and his assistant Mr. Tom Fernekes. These two persons inspired me greatly with the compassion and concern that they showed to the participants in the program.

I find myself in 1997, 20 years later, using many of the techniques that I learned from Bill Garove, and Tom Fernekes in the training that I provide to the staff that I train.

I have been with the State of Arkansas in various training and supervisory capacities since 1974. I am currently in the staff development section at the Conway Human Development Center in Conway, Arkansas, which is about 30 miles from Little Rock. I have never had a greater job than this one. This is a facility that provides residential and educational services to over 600 individuals who are developmentally disabled. There is a staff of over 1200 employees.

I have the great opportunity to provide training to all new employees. I also provide supervisory and management training to supervisory staff and for those employees who possess supervisory potential. I frequently tell the staff and the individuals who live there that God has blessed me to work at a place where I feel like I should be the one paying the state for allowing me the wonderful opportunity to work there with them rather than the state paying me.

The greatest event in my life also occurred in 1974. It was this year that I made the greatest decision that anyone could ever make in their life. The decision to follow Jesus! I had been brought up in the church all of my life but it was on Sunday night, September 1, 1974 around 10:00 P.M. that I surrendered my life to Jesus Christ. That night He saved and sanctified me and baptized and filled me with His precious Holy Ghost. My life has never ever been the same. Elder Lem Williams who is now deceased, was the pastor of the Williams Temple Church of God In Christ in Little Rock which is the place where I got saved and also the church where I grew up in after moving to Little Rock in 1963 with my family. The church that I attended in Stuttgart, Arkansas, before moving to Little Rock was the Benton Temple Church of God In Christ where the late Elder C. L. Benton was the pastor. He was also my uncle. It was at these two historic places in my life that the stage was set for September 1, 1974 to take place. It was the greatest day of my life!

The year of 1974 was about to end but God would not allow it to before allowing me to accept the call to the gospel ministry. On December 29, 1974 on a Sunday afternoon around 1:00 P.M. also at Williams Temple Church of God In Christ, I publicly accepted God's call for me to preach the gospel of Jesus Christ. The late Elder Herman Garrett had just preached a powerful and moving youth day sermon. Upon rising from my seat to make remarks concerning the message, I was immediately and overwhelmingly engulfed by the Holy Ghost as I attempted to make remarks concerning the message. The Spirit of God spoke through me the words preach, preach, preach! After these words were uttered I was caught up and led by the Spirit of God into the pulpit before and in the presence of a great cloud of witnesses. I had felt the call to preach after getting saved on September 1, 1974 but I had asked God to make it so plain to me that there would be no room for any doubt as to whether this is what He wanted me to do. On that very eventful winter Sunday afternoon He left me no room for doubt. I have no doubt whatsoever that I have been touched by the Master's hand and called to preach the gospel.

To those who have not given your life to Jesus Christ I strongly encourage you to do so before it is too late. God loves you and it is His desire that you be saved. Giving my life to Jesus was the greatest decision that I have ever made in my life. My life has never been the same since September 1, 1974. To those who have given your life to Jesus I encourage you to hold on and be strong and of good courage and don't let nobody turn you around!

Romans chapter 10 and verses 9-10 says:

(9) That if thou shalt confess with thy mouth the Lord Jesus, and shalt believe in thine heart that God hath raised him from the dead, thou shalt be saved.

(10) For with the heart man believeth unto righteousness; and with the mouth confession is made unto salvation.

Acts 1:8 says:

(8) But ye shall receive power, after that the Holy Ghost is come upon you: and ye shall be witnesses unto me both in Jerusalem, and in all Judea, and in Samaria, and unto the uttermost part of the earth.

So, this is a great opportunity and a great time for you to PUT SOME GRATITUDE IN YOUR ATTITUDE!®

UPDATE ON THE WORLDWIDE TOUR
January 1996 - January 2006

In January 1996 God told me to start a worldwide tour to share my testimony of the miraculous healing that He gave me from the rare disease of the muscles and skin called dermatomyositis. I started it as He directed me to. I went two blocks from home proclaiming the worldwide tour that God had directed me to start. After that I went about five miles from home and then gradually further and further away from home proclaiming the worldwide tour. At this time I had only traveled within the state of Arkansas on the worldwide tour. My critics then set in and began to question the validity of my claims by asking if it was true that I was on a worldwide tour but still was within the confines of Arkansas. I boldly let them know that it was absolutely true because God told me that I was on one even though I hadn't been outside of Arkansas. I let them know that "a journey of ten thousand miles must first begin with one step". I let them know that I had made that first step and that I would let nobody turn me around! I continued to travel all over Arkansas sharing my testimony at various churches and to different groups. Not long after I proclaimed the worldwide tour I woke up one morning and God told me to start calling myself a Motivational Speaker and to make up some brochures with information in it about my healing and send them around the world. Ron Barnett helped me to develop my first motivational brochures in 1997 and he encouraged me to get them copyrighted and I did. After getting my brochures made up I began to pass them out everywhere that I went and I also began to look around for addresses to send them to. God first led me to look around my house for addresses on products that I use on a daily basis such as cereal boxes, orange juice containers, the internet and anywhere else that I could find an address to send a brochure to. I began to get responses from some of them such as a letter from President Bill Clinton acknowledging that he had received my information. I also received a letter from Minute Maid orange juice saying how blessed they were to get my information. They also enclosed some free coupons for Minute Maid orange juice. Some of the places were not so happy to receive the brochure and they let me know by returning the brochures to me and asking me not to send anymore to them. I did as they asked me to but I didn't let that stop me from sending them to other places. I knew that I would have to be patient and strong and of good courage and that God would work things out for me! Whenever I would receive a brochure that someone had sent back to me I would immediately take it out of the envelope and would mail it to someone else the same day.

In August 1996 a good friend and former co-worker, Sharon Mohammed and I conducted a motivational seminar together at the Austin Hotel in Hot Springs, AR. There I shared my testimony of the miraculous healing that God gave me from the rare muscle disease. At the seminar I met several wonderful people including Lisa Gamble from Hope, AR, Melinda Davis from Pine Bluff, AR and Mary Grant from DeQueen, AR. They told me how much they enjoyed me sharing my testimony with them about my miracle. Mary said that she was going back to her church and tell her pastor Elder E.A. Edwards and his wife, Sister Betty Edwards about me. Within a few weeks I received a call from her stating that she had told her pastor and his wife about me and that he had given his permission for me to come in October 1996 to speak at a program at their church. I gladly accepted the invitation and took the worldwide tour to DeQueen, AR. Soon after that I received a call from Pastor Edwards requesting that I bring the worldwide tour back to DeQueen in December 1996 to conduct a three night end of the year revival service. On my way to DeQueen I observed a sign that said "Broken Bow, Oklahoma 23 miles". I remembered what my critics had said about the worldwide tour still being conducted only in Arkansas. Before church that night I decided to take the worldwide tour over in to

Oklahoma so that I could help silence my critics. I parked my car and walked the streets of Broken Bow, OK, sharing my testimony and inviting people to the revival in DeQueen. Crowds of people gathered around me as I walked through the streets and neighborhoods. After that I thanked them for their kindness and I returned to DeQueen to begin the first night of the revival. As I sat in the church I began to see people come in that I had met earlier in the day over in Oklahoma. About two carloads of them came to hear me preach and several of them got saved that night. When I returned to Little Rock I began to tell people that not only had God blessed me to take the worldwide tour all over Arkansas but He had just blessed me to take it to another state! I conducted year end revival services at the Lewis Temple Church of God In Christ in DeQueen, AR every year from December 1996 until December 2003. It was a wonderful opportunity and I met so many wonderful people!

In June 1997 I was asked by Mr. Bob Clark, former Superintendent of the Conway Human Development Center where I work to conduct a motivational seminar at a regional training conference called "Beyond The Borders". This conference was held in August 1997. It is sponsored by CHDC and people who work with persons with developmental disabilities from surrounding states to Arkansas were invited to attend. The conference had been going on a few years prior to the time that he asked me to speak. I was chairman of the equipment committee and already knew a lot of the people that attended each year. When they realized that I had been asked to speak they were very happy for me and said that they would attend my session. The session went great! I got to share my testimony during the seminar and people had to be turned away from it because there was not enough room for everyone who wanted to attend. After the session two ladies named Alicia Arthur and Sharyln Winstead from Rolla Regional Center in Rolla, MO came up to me and asked me if I would come to speak at their center. I told them that I would be happy to. In April 1998 I flew to St. Louis, MO, rented a car and took the worldwide tour to Rolla and Columbia, MO.

Mr. Clark asked me to speak at Beyond the Borders again in August 1998. Again there was an overwhelming response to my session. After this session several ladies from Tennessee asked me to come to their places of employment to conduct some seminars. In November 1998 I flew to Nashville, TN and took the worldwide tour to Columbia, TN where Donna English and Judy Anderson work and to Gallatin, TN where Wanda Bush and Peggy Gardner work. During this time I also got a call from Jo Battle and Jo Nalley from Jonesboro, AR. Jo Battle asked me to come to Jonesboro and do a motivational seminar for Crowley's Ridge Development Council Head Start program. She let me know that there were Head Start programs all over the country who could use my services. After she told me this I began to inquire about how I could get in touch with those programs. I was told that there was a National Head Start Yellow Page directory that listed all of the programs within the United States. I was able to locate a copy of the directory and proceeded to send a copy of my motivational brochures to nearly all of them. Slowly I began to get inquiries from some of them. My name started to circulate among persons who worked in Head Start programs all over the country.

In June of 2000 I spoke at a Region VI Head Start Conference in Dallas, TX. There were several hundred persons from different states that attended this conference. The session went great! After my session I stayed around for about three hours meeting and conversing with people from other states. After the conference I received a call to do a seminar for a Head Start program in the Tulsa, OK area for the end of June. A few days later I received a call to speak at a Head Start Conference in Albuquerque, NM for July 2000. I spoke at another Head Start Program located in the Albuquerque, NM area in August of 2000. Also in the summer of 2000 my wife and I flew to Houston, TX and then drove to Galveston, TX to celebrate our 27th wedding anniversary. We stayed in a hotel which gave us a great view of the Gulf of Mexico! We had a great time! In October 2000 I spoke at a graduation ceremony in Denver, CO, at Pima Medical

Institute. My sister-in-law Joyce Hawthorne recommended me to her instructors. She graduated from their Medical Office Assistant Program. My wife went with me and we had a great time in Denver visiting Joyce, her husband Rev. Jimmy Hawthorne and their children Adrienne, Gina and Jim. God blessed me to make significant accomplishments on the world-wide tour for the year of 2000.

In the year of 2001 God blessed me to travel to Cleveland, OH; Flint, MI; Detroit, MI; Fargo, ND; Minneapolis and Detroit Lakes, MN; Dallas, TX; and Alexandria, Shreveport, Baton Rouge, and New Orleans, LA. My New Orleans speaking engagement was on Saturday, September 15, 2001. We all know about the destruction of the World Trade Center that occurred on September 11, 2001 and all air traffic was brought to a standstill. The planes started back flying on Friday, September 14th and I was on a flight to New Orleans on Saturday, September 15th. God blessed the worldwide tour to continue! There were some who tried to discourage me from flying but I told them if the planes were flying that I was flying also! I was met at the airport by a good friend of mine, Robel Howard, who drove me to my speaking engagement, took me to Church with him on Sunday morning and he and his wife Freida cooked dinner for me and I flew back to Little Rock on Sunday night September 16th. I had a great time and on each flight to and from New Orleans I had the opportunity to go first class because there were only about 20 people on each flight.

In 2002 the worldwide tour continued to Mexico. Another country! I also traveled to West Palm Beach, Boca Raton, Ft. Lauderdale and Miami, FL. I also went to Los Angeles and San Diego, CA. While in the Los Angeles International Airport I met the former television host Art Linkletter. I walked up to him and introduced myself shared my testimony with him and gave him one of my motivational brochures. He encouraged my worldwide tour and my motivational speaking career and told me that I needed to hire me an agent! My wife went with me on this trip to Los Angeles, I went to Los Angeles twice in 2002. On one of the trips I had to speak at a Head Start Conference and on the other trip my wife and I got to visit with my sister Mary Johnson and her husband Lindy. We also got to meet her son Elder Jerry Lyons and his wife Felecia and my cousin Ruth Moton. This was our first visit to California and we had a super time visiting several of the cities in the area and the beautiful ocean fronts. While in San Diego I got to visit with some longtime friends from Arkansas, Doyle and Beatrice Jenkins, their daughter Mitri Ann and her son Brian.

2002 also took me to Pasadena, CA; South Padre Island, TX; Detroit, MI; Springfield, MO; Seattle, Tacoma, and Olympia, WA. While in the Seattle Airport I saw a friend of mine from Arkansas. Her name is Tamara Satterfield. We both were surprised to see each other at the same airport so far away from home. God also took the worldwide tour to San Antonio, and Carrizo Springs, TX; ST. Louis, MO; Tulsa and Oklahoma City, OK and to New York City and Brooklyn, NY.

While in Oklahoma City I visited the memorial site where the bombing of the Federal building took place. This brought back a lot of memories because I was at home recuperating from my illness when I saw pictures on television as the events unfolded on April 19, 1995. A good friend of mine, Mr. J.J. Pace, came by that day to take me out to lunch. This was a very sad day for all of us. Mr. Pace and his daughter Vicki Cowley have been a great source of encouragement to me as I have traveled on the worldwide tour.

While in New York City I visited the site where the World Trade Center once stood and where thousands of people were killed on a day that we will never forget, September 11, 2001. This was another very sad day for all of us. While in the New York City area I went over to Brooklyn, NY where I visited the church of a good friend of mine, the world renowned gospel singer Rev. Timothy Wright! I was blessed to share my testimony at his church and we all had a great time! While at La Guardia Airport in New York I turned around and saw some people that looked very familiar to me. I walked over to them and found out that it was some good friends of mine from Little Rock, AR, Mrs. Consevella James, her husband and their children. While also at La Guardia Airport I saw a gentleman that also looked familiar to me. I walked over to him and introduced myself to him and found out that he was the world renowned gospel singer, Donnie McClurkin. I also shared my testimony with him and gave him one of my brochures on Put Some Gratitude in Your Attitude!® 2002 was a great year and God blessed me to go to many places and to meet many people!

2003 was another great year for the worldwide tour! I traveled to Orlando, Tampa, ST. Petersburg, Clearwater and Daytona Beach, FL. My wife went with me on this trip and we had a wonderful time. I also traveled to Omaha, NE; Sioux City and Demoines, IA; Atlanta, Albany, and Macon, GA; Tallahassee, FL; Sioux City, SD; Denver, and Colorado Springs, CO; Birmingham, and Gasden, AL; Alexandria, VA and Washington, DC. 2003 also carried me to Baltimore, MD, Philadelphia, PA and over into the state of New Jersey. Other places that God blessed the worldwide tour to visit included Buffalo, Rochester, and Niagara Falls, NY and over into Canada. My wife also went with me on this trip and we had a super time! Other places visited in 2003 included Boston, MA; Keene, NH; Portland, ME; Burlington, VT; Hartford, CT; Providence, RI; and Memphis, TN. Everywhere I go I pass out my motivational brochures and share my testimony about the miraculous healing that God gave me from the rare muscle disease dermatomyositis.

2003 was not only a great year for the worldwide tour but it was also a very eventful year! On August 14, 2003, shortly after getting picked up from the Detroit Metro Airport by my brother Charles Johnson and his wife, Diane, a news bulletin came across the radio that a blackout had just occurred over the entire northeast section of the country, which included Detroit, MI. I had flown to Detroit to do a seminar on Put Some Gratitude In Your Attitude!® for a local Head Start Program. As we continued to monitor the car radio, we began to realize the seriousness of the report as we noticed traffic began to back up and people began to rush to stores to buy flashlights, generators, food and gasoline. We stopped at a local hardware store to buy flashlights, batteries and to inquire about generators, but there were so many people there and tempers began to flare because people began to panic. Before the blackout I had told Charles and Diane that I was planning to spend my first night in town in a hotel so that I could be close to my training site for the next day and that I would spend my second night in town with them. Of course, even before the blackout they had tried to convince me to spend both nights with them but to no avail. Even after being aware of the blackout my plans were still to just spend one night with them until they took me by the hotel and I saw no lights whatsoever. I went inside the hotel to see if there were any generator powered lights operating, but was told that they were not. As I observed strangers walking around with flashlights and there were no lights in the rooms, I immediately changed my plans. I told Charles and Diane that if I had to be in the dark I would rather be in dark with my relatives rather than with strangers. We then got back into the vehicle and went to their house. We were all in the dark but I felt safer than I would have at the hotel. Charles took me to the training site the next day, and as we suspected, the training had been cancelled because of the blackout! I wasn't able to fly out of Detroit until three days later because the flights had been cancelled. In spite of all of this, I had a super time in Detroit. We had to drive for miles outside of Detroit on an empty tank of gas and when we finally found a gas station that had lights and gasoline we had to wait in line for about three hours to get gasoline but we still had some "Gratitude In Our Attitude"! Charles and Diane still tease me about my plans to just spend one night with them when I ended up staying three nights because of the blackout!

One week later on August 21, 2003, another very memorable incident occurred. I had just arrived in Cheyenne, WY, for a speaking engagement the next day at a local Head Start Program. I decided that I would stop and eat before checking into the hotel. I checked into the hotel around 6:00 P.M. but around 9:00 P.M. I had gotten deathly ill from the food that I had eaten or from the high elevation or a combination of both. I became very nauseated and very weak. While in the bathroom standing over the sink I became so sick and weak that I passed out and fell backwards onto the bathtub and injured my back. When I came to I could barely get up and I could barely walk. I laid down for awhile and began to feel worse. I concluded that I needed to seek medical attention. By this time it is around 10:15 P.M. I was in excruciating pain but I had some "Gratitude In my Attitude" I hobbled downstairs, and explained to the desk clerk what had happened and asked her to call 911 for me. Before leaving the room to go downstairs I grabbed a stack of my brochures on Put Some Gratitude In Your Attitude!® because I remembered that I was still on the worldwide tour even though I was sick! She called 911 and within moments I began to hear sirens from a distance and I knew that help was on the way. The first to arrive was the fire department and then the ambulance. I was still alert and very talkative as usual. They asked me several questions and then loaded me into the ambulance for the trip to the hospital emergency room. Before allowing them to take off, I expressed my gratitude to them for responding so quickly and for being so nice to me. They were trying to close the back door to the ambulance, but my feet kept them from doing so because I was reaching some of my brochures to them that said, Put Some Gratitude In Your Attitude!® I told them that they already had "some gratitude in their attitudes" but I asked them to share the brochures with their co-workers. Finally, after I quit talking and allowed them to close the door, we were off to the hospital. As they rolled me into the emergency room on the stretcher, I began to converse with the hospital staff and I flashed victory signs and I told them that God would pull me through this! Some began to wonder about my mental stability and pondered as to whether they needed to admit me to the top floor that is reserved for their special patients who may need some extra attention. I let them know that All Is Well And Then Some...No Matter What!® I told them to Put Some Gratitude in Your Attitude!® We all had a great time. It made being sick a lot easier!

As we entered the treatment room I was still very ill but I still conversed with the doctors, nurses, and staff. I praised God in the midst of my illness. The doctor saw that in spite of how sick I was that I was still praising God. As he treated me he asked me if I minded if he prayed for me. I hastily agreed and he laid hands on me and petitioned God on my behalf. I needed all the prayer that I could get because I had a seminar to do from 8:00 A.M. to 4:00 P.M. the next day. They ran tests and took x-rays of my back and found that nothing was broken but that my back was badly bruised. It is now around 11:30 P.M. and I am still very nauseated and very weak. At this time I felt that it may be a good idea to call my wife and let her know what was going on. She immediately became concerned about my well-being and asked me if she needed to catch the next plane out of Little Rock to Cheyenne. I thanked her but told her that I was confident that I would be fine. I was discharged from the emergency room at 3:30 A.M. They wrote me two prescriptions for some medication. The only problem was that my rental car was at the hotel and I had no transportation back to the hotel. They called and paid for a taxi for me. I thanked the hospital staff for taking such good care of me. The taxi driver was really nice to me also. He took me by a local Walgreens to get my prescriptions filled and then took me to my hotel. As we rode I shared my testimony with him and gave him one of my brochures on Put Some Gratitude in Your Attitude!® I thanked him for his kindness! By this time it is 4:30 A.M. My seminar is scheduled from 8:00 A.M. until 4:00 P.M. today, August 22nd. I laid down for an hour and a half and then was back up at 6:00 A.M. to get ready for my training session. I was limping and still in a lot of pain from the fall on the bathtub but I was not as nauseated. I was confident that God would give me the victory! While getting ready I received a call from my brother Charles in Detroit. Somehow he had gotten the news about my situation and wanted to know if I needed to cancel my session but I told him that "ALL IS WELL" and that I had some "Gratitude In My Attitude!" I arrived at the training site before most of the staff did. I explained to them what had happened and they asked me if I wanted to cancel it, but I let them know that I had come too far to cancel it. I thanked them but I told them that God would get me through it! Things went well until lunch time and I got very nauseated again and I was still limping and in a lot of pain. Again I told them that I was counting on God to get me through the rest of the day. At 4:00 P.M. God had gotten me through the entire day! Even though I was sick God blessed me and got me through the whole day and the training went absolutely wonderful. Everyone at the Head Start Program in Cheyenne was so nice to me! I stayed an extra day and took the worldwide tour to some other cities in Wyoming. When I returned to Little Rock I scheduled an appointment with my family doctor, Dr. Jim Morse. Dr. Morse is an excellent physician! He checked me out real good and said that nothing was broken but my back was bruised pretty bad. God brought me through that and I have not had any problems with it since. Praise God!!

Another exciting event occurred on September 6, 2003 while in Baltimore, MD, on the worldwide tour. About 3:00 A.M. I was awakened by the fire alarm at the hotel where I was staying. I jumped up, got dressed in about five seconds, grabbed a stack of brochures on Put Some Gratitude in Your Attitude!® and ran out of the hotel. I checked the front desk to see if it was a real evacuation; I found out that smoke had been detected on my floor. I then ran back upstairs and went from room to room knocking on doors at 3:12 A.M. telling people that they needed to evacuate. They looked at me like they thought I was a little strange, and they were slow to evacuate. I then ran back outside and watched as the fire department evaluated the situation. They determined that it was not very serious and that someone had been smoking in a non smoking room, and that is what triggered the alarm. We were allowed to return to our rooms around 3:55 A.M. While outside I began to converse with people and shared my testimony with them and passed out some brochures on Put Some Gratitude in Your Attitude!® In the process of talking to different people, I met a gentleman from Arkansas who now works for the federal government in Washington, D.C. We found out that we know some of the same people who live in Arkansas. Praise God for the opportunity to be evacuated!

Another exciting event in 2003 occurred in Washington, D.C. while driving down Pennsylvania Avenue near the U.S. Capitol. I observed what appeared to be the Presidential Motorcade. As I took a closer look I realized that it was and I was able to get a glimpse of President George Bush as the secret service agents ushered him to the waiting limousine.

The worldwide tour continued to make progress in 2004. February 2004 led me to Dallas, TX to speak at North Lake Community College, where a great friend work that I went to college with. Her name is Adrienne "Drina" Settles. She had come across one of my motivational brochures on Put Some Gratitude in Your Attitude!® and she called me to set up a speaking engagement. It went great! The next stop was to Ft. Smith, AR, to speak at a conference for the Arkansas Chapter of the National Association of Social Workers. A good friend of mine, Annette Woodruff, invited me to speak. It was a great conference. At this conference, former Governor of Arkansas, Senator Dale Bumpers was also on to speak. I had the opportunity to meet him for the first time. I had heard him speak before, but I had never personally met him. Senator Bumpers spoke at the commencement exercise when I received my Master's degree from the University of Central Arkansas in Conway on August 10, 1973, while he was governor. He encouraged the graduates to remain in Arkansas because of the great opportunities for everyone. After having unusual difficulty finding things to be as he said they were, I wrote him a letter and let him know the problems that I was having securing employment with the State of Arkansas. He wrote me back and let me know that he had contacted several state agencies and told them about me. Within a short period of time I was employed by the State of Arkansas and have been for the last 31 years. I got a chance to personally thank him for doing that for me. He was very happy that I shared that with him.

In July 2004 my wife and I celebrated 31 years of marriage in New Orleans, LA, and Biloxi, MS. We had a great time! 2004 also took me to Monroe, LA; Traverse City, MI; Albuquerque, Santa Fe and Los Lunas, NM; Indianapolis, IN; Danville, IL, Knoxville, TN and over into parts of North Carolina. The world-wide tour continued with a speaking engagement for the Pennsylvania State Head Start Association in Harrisburg, PA. I also went to Baltimore, MD, and Washington, D.C. My wife accompanied me to these cities, and we had a great time!

God also gave me the wonderful opportunity in 2004 to meet a great, internationally known motivational speaker who had inspired me during my illness through his tapes and had helped to inspire me to become a motivational speaker even though I had never met him. His name is Les Brown! I met him on August 3, 2004, at Hartsfield-Jackson International Airport in Atlanta, GA. We had been on the same flight and didn't know it. I recognized him, and went up to him, and introduced myself, shared my testimony and gave him one of my brochures on PUT SOME GRATITUDE IN YOUR ATTITUDE!® We chatted for a few minutes and I thanked him for having encouraged me through his tapes and we went our separate ways. This was a great opportunity to meet such a distinguished gentleman!

Also in 2004 I received a call from Fairbanks, Alaska. They had received one of my motivational brochures and wanted to know when I could come there and do a seminar on PUT SOME GRATITUDE IN YOUR ATTITUDE!®

In 2004 I was blessed to get some tee shirts made up with PUT SOME GRATITUDE IN YOUR ATTITUDE!® printed on them. They have been a great success and people are wearing them all over the country! I normally wear one as I travel through airports from coast to coast! Many people have stopped me and told me how much they were blessed by seeing the slogan! Those who don't say anything look intently upon the words. I have received many positive reports from people around the country who receive the same type of compliments when they wear their shirts. To God be the glory!

2005 arrived and God has blessed me again to take the world-wide tour to many cities. The first stop on the 2005 tour was to

Mackinaw Island, MI, to speak to a Foster Grandparent and Senior Companion Conference. This was a very unique trip because I flew in to Pellston, MI, and had to catch a ferry across Lake Huron to get to the Island. There are no cars allowed on the Island except for emergency vehicles. The mode of transportation is horse and buggy, bicycle or on foot. I stayed at the Grand Hotel and had a grand time! Other places visited in 2005 were State College, Phillipsburg, Bedford, Altoona, and Pittsburg, PA.

My wife and I celebrated our 32nd wedding anniversary in July 2005 by flying to West Palm Beach, FL. We stayed at a hotel overlooking the Atlantic Ocean. We had a great time! We also traveled to Boca Raton, Ft. Lauderdale, Miami and Riviera Beach, FL. While in Riviera Beach we met a wonderful lady named Ms. Alma Hill. While in the Palm Beach area we ate at a great restaurant by the name of Tom's Ribs. There we met Tom Jr. and his sister Sandra and the great employees at the restaurant!

I also traveled to New Orleans and Robert, LA, in 2005. I flew to New Orleans and spoke outside of New Orleans in Robert, LA. I spoke at Regina Coeli Child Development Center Head Start Conference on August 16, 2005. I met a lot of wonderful people at RCCDC! They included Ms. Judy Loyde, Executive Director, Ms. Shawn Fox and many others. This was two weeks before Hurricane Katrina came to the area. God blessed me to do a seminar on PUT SOME GRATITUDE IN YOUR ATTITUDE!® I still keep in touch with them, and they are still keeping the faith!

2005 also took me to Springfield, MO; Baton Rouge, LA, St. Louis, MO, and to Southern Illinois University at Carbondale Head Start Program. There I met Ms. Joyce Guy, Ms. Mary Sikorski, Ms. Cathy Reed and many other wonderful people! After speaking in Carbondale, IL I traveled to San Antonio, TX and on to Carrizo Springs, TX, where I spoke at a Head Start conference for the Community Services Agency of South Texas. I was invited by Mr. David Ojeda, Executive Director, and Ms. Maria Flores. This was my third time speaking to this group! Other wonderful people that I have met at CSA are Ms. Saldivar, Yvette Reyes, Xavier Flores and many more!

In August 2005 I was in Dallas, TX, to speak at the Dallas Chapter of the Federally Employed Women Conference. I was invited by Ms. LaTanya Kelley, the president, and Ms. Peggy Kirkwood. It was a great conference and I met many wonderful people such as Ms. Patricia Borens-Jackson, Dr. Katie Arnette, Mr. Leon McCowan and his wife, Curtistene, and many others.

In November 2005 I was invited to speak at the State Conference for the Indiana Foster Care and Adoptive Parent Association. I was invited by Ms. Christina Morrison, Executive Director and Mr. Steve Brown, State President. It was also a great conference and I met a lot of wonderful people.

The 2005 worldwide tour also took me to Sault Ste. Marie, MI. This is reported to be the oldest city in Michigan. There I observed the "SOO Locks". The "SOO Locks" have been referred to as one of the great wonders of the world and is still considered to be the largest waterway system on earth. Hugh ships from all over the world go through the locks at Sault Ste. Marie to connect with the Great Lakes and other bodies of water here in the United States. It was very interesting to watch! I also traveled to West Virginia during 2005.

Another interesting event took place in 2005 while my brother Charles Johnson and his wife, Diane, were on a cruise in Alaska. Charles was wearing a tee shirt that I had given him with PUT SOME GRATITUDE IN YOUR ATTITUDE!® on it. Someone came up to him in Alaska and wanted to know if he was "Roy Johnson's" brother. God is blessing the word to get out!

December 2005 was the eleventh anniversary of the major illness that I experienced in December 1994. Our God is an awesome God! I am healed!! The last eleven years have been the best years that I have ever had in my life, inspite of what I have gone through, because it is what I have gone through that has made it so great! Out of all that I have been through I still have joy! The illness provided the opportunity for me to travel from coast to coast to tell people to PUT SOME GRATITUDE IN YOUR ATTITUDE!® After God miraculously healed me of dermato-myositis, the rare disease of the muscles and skin, I have not had any problems at all as a result of the muscle disease. I am completely healed and delivered from it. I am not on any medication for it, and there are no signs that I have ever had it. As a result of having gone through the illness, my faith in God is deeper, my determination is stronger and my desire to please God is more intense than it has ever been before. To God be the glory!! I have had annual checkups for the last ten years, and my results continue to come back "muscle disease free"! Praise God!

Dr. Christopher Adams was my rheumatologist during my illness, but he has since moved out of state. He did a wonderful job of caring for me, and I really hated to see him leave the state. My new rheumatologist is Dr. Columbus Brown III. I have visited his office a couple of times for checkups and "ALL IS WELL!" Dr. Brown is also a great physician! His dad, Columbus Brown Jr. and I attended the same school in Stuttgart, AR.

On Friday, December 30, 2005, I went by St. Vincent Infirmary Medical Center in Little Rock to celebrate the eleventh anniversary of being admitted to the hospital. I was admitted on Friday, December 30, 1994. I was so sick that many people thought that I would not live through the night, but God told me to start a midnight revival service my first night in the hospital. This lasted for the entire 35 days that I was hospitalized. The days of the week and the dates of the month are exactly the same as they were eleven years ago. This is what made the visit extra special! I went straight to the floor that I was on, 3 NW. I stopped at the nurses' desk to see if anyone was there that took care of me eleven years ago. No one was there that took care of me, but they said they had heard about me! I shared my testimony with them and then went to room 2344, where I spent 35 days from December 30, 1994 to February 2, 1995. I walked in the room, looked around and had a flashback to eleven years ago. I began to praise and to magnify God for healing me of the rare muscle disease that almost took my life. I shared my testimony with almost everyone that I saw as I left the hospital, whether they wanted to hear it or not. This visit to the hospital was the highlight of the eleventh anniversary of my illness.

Much of December 2005 was spent wishing everyone a MERRY CHRISTMAS AND HAPPY NEW YEAR! rather than Happy Holidays because: "JESUS IS THE REASON FOR THE SEASON" AND "WITHOUT CHRIST THERE WOULD BE NO CHRISTMAS"!!

Saturday night December 31, 2005, was spent at my home church, Williams Temple Church of God In Christ in Little Rock, AR, where Elder Jewel Withers Jr. is pastor. My wife, Marie, my daughter, Eboni Johnson, and my granddaughter Keyona "KiKi" Johnson also went with me. We praised God for 2005 and thanked Him for the success of the worldwide tour since January 1996. We praised God as 2005 went out and as 2006 came in.

My good friend Elder Paul Robinson, pastor of Acts 2:4 Church of God In Christ in Little Rock, was the guest speaker. His wife, Sister Carla Robinson, did a super job of directing the choir from their church. Brother Joeson Daniels did a super job of directing the great Williams Temple Choir. The musicians, Joeson Daniels, Jeremy Withers and Sir Withers, did a great job with the music. Some of the ministers from our church who participated in the services were Pastor Jewel Withers, Jr., Elders Donnell Flowers, Chadd Morgan, York Porter, Donald Miller and Minister James Gray. We praised the old year out and the new year in. We had a great time!

There were many people who were a great source of encouragement and inspiration to me during my illness and over the past eleven years. Some of them include: Louis and Wanda Page, Lena Lucas, Willie and Dorothy Page, Joyce Banks, Sandra Sherman, Boyd Hancock, Elmer Strickland, Vada Mosby, Angela Scales, Sheila Maxfield, Joyce Harrington, Mark and Kerry Stitch, and Jimmy Garis. Others include: Sally Sellers, Neal and Margaret Goldsmith, Earnett and Valeria Maltbia, Raymond Lowe, Janice Brown, Stephanie Carter, John Morgan, Michael Banks, Eary Lee, Mona Koonce, Margaret Johnson, Helen Anderson, Joy Weidower, Laura Ealy, Linda Graham, Regina Kellybrew, Julia Groff, Chris Delph, Seth Cunningkin, Miles Shirley and his family and many more people!

My neighbors have always been there to encourage me. Some of them are: Archie and Bertha Lowe, George and Regina Wilford, Jerry and Connie Jackson, Jennie Van Buren, Vernell Ryan, Laverne Ryan, A.C. Wilson and Anthony Brown. I have also received a lot of encouragement from my nephews Everett O. Martindale and Charles Simmons.

January 2006 is here! New Years Day I found myself at University Medical Center in Little Rock with a friend of mine who had taken ill. As I stood in the emergency room treatment area with him, I began to have flashbacks to March 18, 1964. This is the same emergency room that I was brought to when I was run over by a car and nearly killed almost 42 years ago. I had to stop and Praise God for allowing me to still be alive and well and not experiencing any side effects from the accident!

January 2006 is the tenth anniversary of the worldwide tour. I started the worldwide tour in January 1996. God has truly blessed the tour over the last ten years as I have traveled to nearly all of the fifty states, to over 200 cities, and have traveled to other countries sharing my testimony of the miraculous healing that God gave me from the rare muscle disease dermatomyositis!

On Sunday, January 8, 2006, I traveled to Elect Temple Church of God In Christ in Benton, Arkansas, where Elder Willie Barnes Jr. is the pastor. I went there to celebrate the tenth anniversary of the worldwide tour. This is where it officially started on Sunday January 14, 1996. I thought that it would be very befitting to go back to where it all started ten years ago. Pastor Barnes gave me an opportunity to share my testimony. We all had a great time! I passed out some of my brochures on PUT SOME GRATITUDE IN YOUR ATTITUDE!®

On Monday, January 9, 2006, while at the Little Rock National Airport, I had the opportunity to meet former Presidential candidate in the 2004 election, General Wesley Clark. I recognized him and went over and introduced myself and gave him a brochure on PUT SOME GRATITUDE IN YOUR ATTITUDE!® It was great meeting him!

On Thursday, January 12, 2006, while at the Little Rock Public Library, I had the opportunity to meet Ms. Susan McDougal, a friend of President and Mrs. Clinton. I recognized her and went over and introduced myself and gave her a brochure on PUT SOME GRATITUDE IN YOUR ATTITUDE!® It was great meeting her also.

On Sunday, January 15, 2006 I continued celebrating the tenth anniversary of the worldwide tour by visiting the Rosedale Church of God In Christ in Little Rock, where Elder Raymond Savage is the pastor. Elder Savage and his wife Mother Lee Ollie Savage have been a great inspiration to my ministry. I was invited back for Sunday night service to preach. My subject was PUT SOME GRATITUDE IN YOUR ATTITUDE!® We had a great time!

On Sunday, January 22, 2006, I continued to celebrate the tenth anniversary of the worldwide tour by visiting the Holy Benton Temple Church of God In Christ in Stuttgart, Arkansas where the Supt. Lawrence O'Neal is the pastor. He and I grew up together at this church over 45 years ago. He was away but his assistant minister, Elder Steve Mullins, allowed me to share my testimony. Everyone had a great time!

I continued the tenth anniversary worldwide tour celebration by returning back to my home church, which is the Williams Temple Church of God In Christ in Little Rock, where Elder Jewel Withers, Jr. is the pastor. He preached a powerful message on Sunday morning, February 5, 2006, and associate minister, Elder Donald Miller preached another powerful message on Sunday night! I had an opportunity to share my testimony and I expressed to them that God had let me know that He has great blessings in store in 2006 for the worldwide tour! To God be the glory! I have got some "GRATITUDE IN MY ATTITUDE" and I must tell God "Thank You" for all the things that He has done for me!

I am reminded of a passage of scripture in the book of St. Luke Chapter 17, where there were ten men who had leprosy and they cried out for Jesus to have mercy on them. Jesus healed them but only one returned to give Him thanks. He had some "GRAT-ITUDE IN HIS ATTITUDE"!

I have been to so many places and have met so many wonderful people. PUT SOME GRATITUDE IN YOUR ATTITUDE®! is spreading to all corners of the earth! To God be the glory!! 2006 promises to be another wonderful and exciting year. I already have several engagements scheduled in such places as Dallas, TX, Greenville, SC; Charlotte, NC; Orlando, FL; and many other places. I have received several inquiries for 2006 from places such as Chicago, IL; Charleston, WV; Pittsburgh, PA; San Francisco, CA; Washington, DC; and New York City.

I would like to say a special thanks to all of the wonderful people that I have met over the last ten years who have richly blessed my life.

A special thanks goes out to my wonderful wife, Marie, who has been very supportive of my travels. She goes with me as often as she can but when she can't I can always count on her support!

The worldwide tour has come a long way in ten years but still has a long way to go! As I have stated earlier, "A journey of ten thousand miles must first begin with one step"! I am still taking one step at a time and by the help, the grace, and the mercy of God I will continue the worldwide tour until every ounce of breath is gone from my body and then I will be transcended into another world where I will be in the presence of God, His Son Jesus, the Holy Angels and all those who love His appearing. I want to hear the Lord say "Well done, thou good and faithful servant, thou have been faithful over a few things, now come on up and I will make you ruler over many."

I am reminded of what Paul said in II Timothy Chapter 4 verses 6-8:

(6) For I am now ready to be offered, and the time of my departure is at hand.

(7) I have fought a good fight, I have finished my course, I have kept the faith:

(8) Henceforth there is laid up for me a crown of righteousness, which the Lord, the righteous judge shall give

me at that day: and not to me only, but unto all them also that love his appearing.

I am striving everyday to make this my testimony!

Thanks so much for reading this book, I want to encourage you to keep the faith and don't ever give up. Always be thankful grateful and appreciative to God and to others for what they do for you and always remember to PUT SOME GRATITUDE IN YOUR ATTITUDE!®

ST. VINCENT
INFIRMARY MEDICAL CENTER

May 18, 1995

Dear Reverend Johnson:

I want to thank you for your kind letter to me and to the others involved in your care while a patient at St. Vincent Infirmary Medical Center. It is always gratifying to know that we have met our patient's expectations. I enjoyed reading about you in the recent *Spirit Weekly*. The way I hear it, you provided as much "care" to the staff as they provided to you.

We are very proud of the dedicated staff on 3 NW and the outstanding physicians who cared for you at St. Vincent. It was kind of you to take the time to write.

I trust that your health is continuing to improve. If I personally or any of the staff at St. Vincent can be of assistance to you in the future, please don't hesitate to contact us.

Sincerely,

Thomas L. Feurig
President and
Chief Executive Officer

cc: Marcie Justice and
       Staff of 3 NW

NURSING NEWS

Hospital Stay Uplifts Minister, St. Vincent Staff

Although the disease which gripped his body almost immobilized him, the Rev. Roy Johnson was not going to let it dampen his spirits. Shortly after arriving on 3NW for recuperation and treatment for dermatomyositis, a painful, rare arthritic inflammation of the muscles, he began to "Roy Johnsonize" his room.

Johnson is an avid collector of inspirational quotations and the walls of his hospital room were soon covered with photos, cards, clippings, and notes bearing inspirational messages. Johnson is an associate minister at Williams Temple Church of God In Christ in Little Rock and an employee of the Conway Human Development Center, a division of DHS.

In addition to motivating him, the wall "decorations" are designed to "help people when they come in my room," said Johnson. His favorite quote: "All Is Well."

But Johnson didn't stop there. He also conducted short "revival" prayer services in his room for friends and hospital staff members.

Patrice Clipp, RN, was one of a number of nurses and other staff members who were inspired by Johnson's attitude toward his illness. "He gave back a lot to the staff. He's one of a lost breed, a Good Samaritan," said Clipp.

She said, "Basically, with our help, this man healed himself. That's what nursing is all about; teaching people to be independent and do for themselves."

Nurse Serenda Jordan, LPN II, added, "He's been an inspiration to all of us as he's lifted our spirits and preached, and kept us going."

"I was so sick, but they saw how I maintained my faith in God. God did not allow this to happen to me to make me bitter, but to make me better," Johnson said a few hours before he left the hospital after a 35 day stay that began December 30, 1994. "I'm better because of it. I'm a new man because of this outpouring of love from family and friends and my fellow employees."

He also stressed that the St. Vincent staff "has bent over backwards to help me. I praise God for blessing me with the doctors, nurses and staff at St. Vincent. They've been outstanding in their care for me." He extended his praise to Housekeeping and Food Services. Johnson was particularly impressed by the spaghetti dinners. He said, "The kitchen food has been so good."

He added, "If I were to get sick again, I would want Room 2344. I would recommend St. Vincent to anyone."

Article written by St. Vincent Medical Center staff (1995)

The Zig Ziglar ▨ Corporation

THE TRAINING COMPANY

Zig Ziglar
Chairman

October 1, 1997

Mr. Roy Johnson
Post Office Box 1026
Little Rock, Arkansas 72203

Dear Roy:

Thanks for taking a moment to jot me a note and send some information on what you're doing.

What an exciting story you have to tell, Roy! I know it is truly an inspiration and encouragement to everyone who hears it. I've no doubt but that you did as much toward healing those with whom you came in contact during your hospitalization as did those who ministered to you. What an outstanding opportunity to bring glory to our Lord! Surely He is pleased that you are using your own experience to help others.

God bless you, Roy, and keep up the good work!

SEE YOU <u>OVER</u> THE TOP!

Zig Ziglar

Zig Ziglar

ZZ/lms

ORDER INFORMATION

If you would like to order a book or schedule a speaking engagement, you may contact:

Roy Johnson
Post Office Box 1026
Little Rock, Arkansas 72203

Telephone: 501-562-4488
E-Mail: Roystest@aol.com